ISO 9001 AND SARBANES-OXLEY

Other Paton Press books by William A. Stimson:

Internal Quality Auditing

ISO 9001 AND SARBANES-OXLEY:

A SYSTEM OF GOVERNANCE

William A. Stimson

Paton Press LLC
Chico, CA

Most Paton Press books are available at quantity discounts when purchased in bulk. For more information, contact:

Paton Press LLC
P.O. Box 44
Chico, CA 95927-0044
Telephone: (530) 342-5480
Fax: (530) 342-5471
E-mail: *books@patonpress.com*
Web: *www.patonpress.com*

©2006 by William A. Stimson. All rights reserved.
Printed in the United States of America

10 09 08 07 06 5 4 3 2 1

ISBN-13: 978-1-932828-08-5
ISBN-10: 1-932828-08-7

Library of Congress Cataloging-in-Publication Data

Stimson, William A.
ISO 9001 and Sarbanes-Oxley : A system of governance / William A. Stimson.
p. cm.
Includes bibliographical references and index.
ISBN 1-932828-08-7
1. Corporate governance United States. 2. Business ethics United States. 3. Industrial management Moral and ethical aspects United States. 4. ISO 9001 Standard. 5. Quality control standards United States. 6. Total quality management United States. 7. Corporate governance law and legislation United States. 8. United States Sarbanes-Oxley Act of 2002 Criminal provisions. I. Title.
HD2741.S776 2006
658.4'013--dc22
2005034114

Notice of Rights
No part of this work covered by the copyright herein may be reproduced or used in any form or by any means graphic, electronic, or mechanical, including photocopying, recording, taping, or information storage and retrieval systems without permission in writing from Paton Press LLC.

Notice of Liability
The information in this book is distributed on an "as is" basis, without warranty. Although every precaution has been taken in the preparation of the book, neither the author nor Paton Press LLC shall have any liability to any person or entity with respect to any loss or damage caused or alleged to be caused directly or indirectly by the information contained in this book.

Staff
Publisher .... Scott M. Paton
Editor... Anna Moss
Book design .... Caylen Balmain

DEDICATION

To the families of Leonard Moss of Aurora, Illinois, and Antoine Fauret of Saintonge, France: "If only they had known each other!"

CONTENTS

Preface xi

Chapter 1—Goodwill 1
An Axiom of Goodwill 2
A Philosophy for Business Ethics 2

Chapter 2—Ethics in Business 5
The Case for Ethical Standards 6
A Code of Ethics for Business Management 10

Chapter 3—Contracts, Specifications, and Standards ... 17
Writing the Contract 19
Writing Specifications 22
Writing Standards 23

Chapter 4—Quality Management Systems 27
Governance 27
Performance Standards 28
Quality Management Standards 28

Chapter 5—ISO 9000 Quality Management System 39
Background on Quality Standards 39
Genesis of ISO 9000 40
ISO 9000 in the United States 41
Structure of ISO 9000:2000 42
ISO 9001: A Process Approach 43
GE Fanuc 46
A Final Word 47

Chapter 6—Sarbanes-Oxley 49
Title I: Public Company Accounting Oversight Board 51
Title II: Auditor Independence 52
Title III: Corporate Responsibility 54
Title IV: Enhanced Financial Disclosures 56
Title V: Analyst Conflicts of Interest 57

Title VI: Commission Resources and Authority 57
Title VII: Studies and Reports.. 57
Title VIII: Corporate and Criminal Fraud Accountability 58
Title IX: White-Collar Crime Penalty Enhancements 58
Title X: Corporate Tax Returns.. 59
Title XI: Corpoarate Fraud and Accountability 59

Chapter 7—Sarbanes-Oxley and Governance............. 61
Internal Controls 62
Control Environment 62
Control Activity 63
Monitoring and Measuring 68

Chapter 8—An ISO 9001 Format for Sarbanes-Oxley ... 71
Systems Integration... 72
Statutes and Regulations 76

Chapter 9—Financial Measures of Quality................. 79
Cost of Quality... 81
Inventory 83
Financial Measures 84
The Strategic Cost of Quality 85

Chapter 10—SOX Applied to ISO 9001..................... 87
Title I: Public Company Accounting Oversight Board.................................... 90
Title II: Auditor Independence 91
Title III: Corporate Responsibility 95
Title IV: Enhanced Financial Disclosures.. 96
Title V: Analyst Conflicts of Interest 97
Title VI: Commission Resources and Authority 98
Title VII: Studies and Reports.. 98
Title VIII: Corporate and Criminal Fraud Accountability 98
Title IX: White-Collar Crime Penalty Enhancements 100
Title X: Corporate Tax Returns.. 101
Title XI: Corporate Fraud and Accountability 101

Chapter 11—Conclusions and Recommendations.... 103
Conclusion One: A Unified System of Corporate Governance..................... 104
Conclusion Two: A SOX-Friendly Quality System 104

Financial Condition or Results of Operations... 105
Recommendation One: An ISO 9001 Financial System............................... 105
Recommendation Two: Learn Your Production and
    Service Processes.. 107
The Strategic View.. 111
Summary.. 112

Bibliography 115

Index 117

PREFACE

In the year 2000, U.S. industry witnessed large-scale and widespread theft of investment money. Millions of dollars disappeared into private portfolios, much of it legally. These events contributed to a collapse of the stock market and a furor among U.S. investors and workers. Thousands of people lost their investments, retirement funds, savings for college education—everything their families depended on for the future.

The government's reaction was severe, resulting in widespread arrests, "perp-walks" of CEOs on national TV, charges and indictments, and passage of the Sarbanes-Oxley Act of 2002. Often abbreviated as "SOX," the act focuses on financial controls and rules of disclosure. However, its wording is broad so that its requirements can be extended to service and manufacturing operations as well as finance. This book explores just how the seemingly narrow focus of the law on financial control is expanded.

The interaction between SOX and corporate operations is a two-way mapping: from operations to SOX and from SOX to operations. Assuming in the first case that a company has a formal quality management system (QMS) such as ISO 9001, the QMS structure provides a framework that can help it meet SOX compliance. This book shows how to create a single system that governs independent functions, with ISO 9001 providing the format.

In the second case, SOX may in turn be applied to ISO 9001. The rationale for this application is the cost of quality. If the cost factors are material, or if company operations influence the company's market value, SOX requirements will come into play. Given the purview of SOX and the nature of service and manufacturing operations, it's prudent to consider that the CEO will have to validate both financial and quality controls in the future.

Chapter 1 lays the basis for the entire book. Sarbanes-Oxley is, in fact, a Congressional act with all the authority of the law behind it. ISO 9001 is an international standard with all the prestige of the international industrial world behind it. But all of this force and influence really come down to one thing: how people in the business world treat one another.

The Sarbanes-Oxley Act came into being because of illegal and unethical behavior. Much of the behavior, although unethical, was thought by the perpetrators to be legal. For that reason it was pursued because ethics didn't matter to them—only prison did. Thus, SOX is fundamentally an ethical document because it takes certain human conduct and transfers it from the ethical to the legal domain. To understand the law and to see where it may be applied in the future, one must understand the intent of its many titles and have a firm grasp on the intersection between ethics and the law. Chapter 2 describes this intersection.

This book is about how the Sarbanes-Oxley Act and ISO 9001 fit together. SOX is concerned with the relationship between performers and customers. ISO 9001 is a standard of governance. Chapter 3 brings these issues together by describing three kinds of documents that are closely related to the achievement of any major work: contracts, specifications, and standards. Contracts are agreements between a performer and customer to do something for remuneration. The customer's requirements are described in specifications that are associated with the contract. Then the work of the contract begins, usually under the assumption that it will be done in accordance with a standard of performance for the industry.

Chapter 4 talks about quality management systems. These don't manage quality—quality is a characteristic. They manage performance, and if the performance is done well, quality results. In particular, the relationship between system and standard is clarified. Simply put, a standard is a documented system—pure form. It does nothing, but it enables things to be done well. The system is the implementation of the standard. If properly implemented, the system will work well and get things done to the satisfaction of the customer.

This chapter discusses the characteristics of a QMS, then describes some of the better known and widely used systems. Most of these systems are excellent as standards of performance, but what's needed to meet SOX compliance is a standard of governance.

Chapter 5 discusses ISO 9001 in sufficient detail, enabling the requirements of SOX and the capability of ISO 9001 to be unified in later chapters. The details of ISO 9001 requirements are described down to the level of its clauses so that later a mapping can be made of ISO 9001 clauses to SOX titles. The standard uses a process approach in its organization that gives it the flexibility needed to integrate with other standards or with any process. A case study of the GE Fanuc Corp. of Charlottesville, Virginia, is presented to demonstrate the suitability of ISO 9001 as a standard of governance, working in conjunction with Six Sigma as a standard of performance.

The Sarbanes-Oxley Act is described twice in this book. Chapter 6 describes the eleven titles of the law and as many sections of it as are appropriate to business operations. The law covers a wide spectrum of business activity and is primarily aimed at public companies, that is, corporations under the purview of the Securities and Exchange Commission (SEC). However, title VIII is applicable to all corporations, public and private. SOX doesn't replace existing laws covering the activity of the SEC, but it does reinforce some of them. Chapter 10 revisits the titles briefly, reviewing their purpose for the convenience of the reader, and each relevant section is expanded to show how it's applicable to ISO 9001.

SOX is an act of legislation, not a standard. It states what to do but provides no guidelines on how to do it. Inevitably, the law must work together with standards that can conduct operations within an acceptable framework. SOX specifies a few critical issues, primarily concerning corporate governance and internal controls, but it relies on recognized expertise to define and implement them. The Committee of Sponsoring Organizations of the Treadway Commission, or COSO, was assembled in 1985 at the behest of Congress by James Treadway, chairman of the National Commission on Fraudulent Financial Reporting. COSO is sponsored by five major financial professional associations in the United States: the American Accounting Association, the American Institute of Certified Public Accountants, Financial Executives International, The Institute of Internal Auditors, and the Institute of Management Accountants. Chapter 7 is devoted to describing the concepts of governance and internal controls as defined by COSO, which speaks for the SEC and SOX on these matters.

Chapter 8 is one of the key chapters in this book, following up on the promise of using ISO 9001 as a framework for SOX compliance. It provides charts to aid in mapping a financial accounting system to ISO 9001, and to aid in tracing

COSO action items to ISO 9001. This book is written under the premise that the relationship between SOX and ISO 9001 is reciprocal and that, inevitably, SOX will be applied to ISO 9001. In wording, it already is, and the connection is cost of quality, or COQ. Chapter 9 makes this connection explicit.

COQ is rarely put in terms that might interest top management, which is one of the reasons that quality has so little influence in so many corporations. Chapter 9 addresses a few of the financial measures of quality—terms of productivity and shareholder value. Not only can CEOs easily understand the importance of these metrics, but their connection to SOX becomes explicit. If the corporate financial measures of operations are material, then SOX applies to a company's factory floor and service department, while internal controls are subject to its laws regarding effectiveness and reporting. The strategic view of the cost of quality is analyzed to show how operational costs are translated to financial measures that have meaning to top management.

Chapter 10 is devoted to the other promise of the book—how to adapt ISO 9001 to SOX in those areas within its purview, while achieving a single corporatewide system of governance. Just as in chapter 6, this chapter goes through the 11 titles section by section, explaining the nuances of applicability and how to best integrate the issues, clause by clause. Because none of this requires changes in ISO 9001, certification won't be affected. The strategy primarily calls for members of top management to participate in the QMS of their companies, which may keep them out of prison.

Chapter 11 finalizes the book with two conclusions. It also offers two recommendations that are easy to do and will ensure SOX compliance now and in the future. However, the book also presents a dissertation on the strategic view of the corporation because it isn't frequently implemented at the process level. This discontinuity often creates large inefficiencies that may cause difficulties with SOX auditors. If the inefficiencies are undetected, there's no way of knowing their magnitude or whether their costs are material. A company may be operating outside the law unknowingly, but Sarbanes-Oxley holds it responsible for effective controls.

Conventions

Sometimes in the course of discussion, it's necessary to refer to either a particular part of the book, ISO 9001, or the Sarbanes-Oxley Act. A convention of nomenclature must be used in referencing parts of documents in order to avoid confusion. The names of the different parts of SOX are preempted—the U.S. government calls the major parts "titles" and the minor parts "sections." ISO 9000 also has a formal name for its parts, called "clauses."

These conventions permit certain inferences. A statement about, say, clause 8.2 refers to ISO 9001 whether or not ISO 9001 is mentioned in the same paragraph. Similarly, a statement about section 302 refers to the Sarbanes-Oxley Act. And if only a certain part of a chapter is referred to, it will be made clear which chapter that is.

CHAPTER 1

GOODWILL

This book is about human behavior of a special kind—the relationship of humans in a business environment. Fundamentally, then, it's about ethics. The Greek word *ethos* refers to the character of a thing, and when applied to humans, it's usually concerned with a standard of human conduct. Inescapably, there's a sense of goodness in that standard.

It's asserted that the character of ethics is goodness, which is a primitive concept. It can't be defined or proven, or even agreed upon. What I feel is good may not be viewed as good by another. "Goodness" is a viable idea, but it's impossible to agree on what good is. Therefore, societies look for consensus in determining the meaning of goodness and in defining what good is. It's important to understand that in a given society, the right to define "goodness" belongs to that society and not to the individual. If individuals reserved for themselves the right to define what's good, the result would be anarchy, which is the opposite of organized society. Societies can't exist in anarchy.

Therefore, societies have the right and duty to define standards of conduct that have a basis in goodness. However, in free societies, this right necessarily imposes on individual rights so that a certain amount of latitude follows. Whatever the standard of conduct, the general view has been that ethical behavior is pretty much voluntary. Murder and theft relate to human behavior, so in principle, they're ethical issues as well. But we usually don't think of them that way. They're crimes that our society can't tolerate. So we permit a degree of ambiguity in ethical behavior, defining some actions as crimes and others as simply "not nice." By and large, ethical issues are regarded as those that we either can or cannot follow; we might displease our neighbors, but we won't go to prison.

AN AXIOM OF GOODWILL

There's an old phrase that states: *In terra pax hominibus bonae voluntatis*—"On earth peace to men of goodwill." This wisdom is the first axiom of this book. The corollary is that without goodwill, there can be no peace. The conclusion can then be drawn that goodwill is necessary to the fundamental American right to the pursuit of happiness. I have the right to pursue happiness if I can do so without harming others. This requires that my actions are based on goodwill and good behavior toward others.

Some people argue that good behavior is fine in its place, but that goodness in business is both historically and intrinsically irrelevant. When put succinctly, the law of business is the law of the jungle—survival of the fittest. However, the U.S. Constitution is carefully crafted to disallow such a jungle, offering peaceful alternatives. The purpose of the Sarbanes-Oxely Act is to help ensure that goodness can take place in business, if not voluntarily, then by law.

A PHILOSOPHY FOR BUSINESS ETHICS

Humans are social creatures, banding together for company and security. Anthropologists tell us that human beings were hunters and gatherers for thousands of years. We roamed the earth looking for sustenance.

Then farming was developed. This allowed us to stay in one place where we could gather and store inventory. We stored foodstuffs, clothing, products, and tools to use as needed, leveling out the fat and the lean times. In short, we accumulated resources.

The resources belonged to society. Perhaps one person made shoes, and another, bolts of cloth, but others made different resources to trade with them. Still others did work that allowed producers to continue their craft. And yet others protected the producers from predators. Therefore, the resources belonged to everyone.

As the making and gathering of resources became widespread and continuous, it became necessary to manage them. The question arose: "Who should best manage our resources, the government or private groups?" This question is still being asked and probably always will be.

In the United States, private groups manage society's resources. The private groups are called businesses and have managers who plan and implement the strategic and tactical goals necessary to resource management. They're rewarded generously because the job is both important and difficult.

Nevertheless, the resources belong to society. They're derived from the air, sea, rivers, and earth. One of the admirable things about Japanese culture is that it recognizes the obligation business has to society. For example, Toyota defines quality in terms of benefits to society.[1] Genichi Taguchi defines deviation from the nominal as a "loss to society."[2]

Some societies are established for specific reasons. The United States is devoted to individual liberty. The search for a balance between individual rights and society's rights often spills over into business. How does society protect its resources in this search? It must protect itself by imposing constraints, often through some form of accountability. This book is about such constraints.

REFERENCES

1. Liker, J. K. *The Toyota Way.* New York: McGraw-Hill, 2004.
2. Taguchi, Genichi, Elsayed A. Elsayed, and Thomas Hsiang. *Quality Engineering in Production Systems.* New York: McGraw-Hill, 1989.

CHAPTER 2

ETHICS IN BUSINESS

The Public Company Accounting Reform and Investor Protection Act of 2002, commonly known as the Sarbanes-Oxley Act of 2002, states its rationale very concisely in its opening paragraph: "To protect investors by improving the accuracy and reliability of corporate disclosures made pursuant to the public securities laws, and for other purposes." I wish it could be said that the errors occurring in public disclosures were due to unintentional mistakes, for then they could be reduced through increased training, education, and vigilance. In short, one could approach the problem through a Six Sigma methodology for improvement.

But it has become clear in recent history that many of the disclosure errors are deliberate and shady, lying either in the realm of crime or close to the margin that separates crime from simple regrettable action. How can this be? How can it be that so many business operations take place within this margin? I don't have all the answers, but it's likely that ethical principles aren't drilled into future business leaders and that ethical considerations often get in the way of business profit.

My suspicions may be wrong, but they're not unfounded. One could reasonably conclude that some professions are far more advanced than others in developing an ethical code. In the military, for example, there are severe penalties for unethical behavior. It's understandable in a profession with such a well-established history because they've had time to develop an intricate code of conduct. Without declaring where I think business lies in this spectrum of ethical development, I'll devote this chapter to moving it to the high end.

THE CASE FOR ETHICAL STANDARDS

Productivity dominates the concerns of today's executive management.[1,2] In a *Quality Progress* article, Stephen George goes further, saying that if the field of quality is to get the attention of top management, it must learn to integrate quality initiatives with financial performance.[3]

Paul Palmes and Sandford Liebesman echo this idea in another *Quality Progress* article, saying today's quality professionals are increasingly expected to assume cost effectiveness in business planning.[4] Indeed, strategies such as Six Sigma and lean have already done so.

An intense management focus on productivity can and often has led to legal, moral, and ethical compromises. But ethics are what make the workplace tolerable to employees and the marketplace acceptable to customers. If business is to focus mainly on value-adding activities, then a code of ethics becomes essential. However, the trend in modern industrial society has been to rely on guidance that defines crimes very well, but rarely defines or proscribes any misconduct less than criminal. For example, Kim McMurtry reports gathering evidence in U.S. universities that somewhere between 70–85 percent of students cheat.[5] One might argue that cheating has always been with us, but longevity isn't the criterion for acceptability.

The purpose of adopting ethical standards is to reduce the frequency of unethical behavior by reducing its acceptability. Margaret Fain and Peggy Bates offer many views as to why plagiarism is so prevalent in universities, one of which is that many students feel it's "socially acceptable."[6]

High school and college graduates take their ethical views with them into industry. They find no standard there, either. Everyone relies on the law, but many transgressions are within the law. For example, in the Ford-Bridgestone/Firestone product failure hearings of 2000, most civil suits were directed against the tire manufacturers. Hoyer makes the case that Ford shared equal culpability because its strategic policies failed to recognize its role as an assembler of automobiles as well as a manufacturer.[7] Therefore, it had responsibility for the total product—car and tires.

There's no universally recognized code of business practices or of business ethics. Generally, business codes tend to prohibit discrimination based on race, religion, or gender because such discrimination is now prohibited by law. But many codes fail to address conduct that is legal but has moral or ethical shadings that can lead to a demoralized workplace.

The Basis of an Ethical Standard

Ethics deal with the right and wrong of human conduct. It's an intuitive concept—the courts are full of people debating such issues. Perhaps this is why it has proven so difficult to generate a universal code. Clearly murder is wrong and is universally defined as a crime. But usually, as chapter 1 points out, we use the term "ethical behavior" to refer to conduct that is both legal and will avoid hurting others.

It seems reasonable to turn to quality in search of an ethical basis because it has always been primarily concerned with providing good value to customers. The historic naiveté of quality vis-à-vis market forces enhances its credibility as an honest broker. Yet, you won't find an off-the-shelf ethical standard there, either. Six Sigma and lean are popular quality methodologies, in effect akin to standards, but they're oriented to bottom-line results. This is good for business, but it doesn't preclude, for example, oppressive management behavior. ISO 9001 also falls short as an ethical standard, focusing more on process procedures and job training than on human-to-human behavior. ISO 9004 touches on ethical issues but has no contractual force. You can't revoke a company's ISO 9001 certification for unethical but legal behavior.

However, it's possible to derive a basis for ethical behavior from the tenets of quality, and we can start with W. Edwards Deming's 14 points.[8] About half of them are process-oriented, and about half affect human conduct. The relevant points are:

2. Adopt the new philosophy. We're in a new economic age. Western management must awaken to the challenge, must learn their responsibilities, and take on leadership for change.
6. Institute training on the job.
7. Institute leadership.
8. Drive out fear.
9. Break down barriers between departments.
11. Eliminate quotas.
12. Remove barriers to pride of workmanship.

The meaning and scope of these points are expanded upon in Deming's own writings and elsewhere. In this book, they'll be used to justify a code of conduct.

The Deming View

Deming believed that well-trained employees have a natural inclination to do their best and will do so in an encouraging environment. Tom Watson, the founder of IBM, shared this view. Peter Drucker writes of Watson: "He believed in a worker who saw his own interests as identical to those of the company. He wanted, above all, a worker who used his own mind and experience to improve his job, the product, the process, and the company."[9] Deming expressed his conviction in the goodness of human toil in his fourteen points. The essence of the points can be condensed in three notions: employee skill, empowerment, and the absence of fear.

Skill is achieved by training and education, and provides employees with pride of performance and the confidence to make decisions about their tasks. Empowerment gives them the authority to do so, while fear takes it all away.

Skill

Skill is developed through training—pure and simple. From neurosurgery to piano tuning, the more training and education one receives, the greater the skill level. Of course, given the same amount of training, some performers are better than others, and we see this demonstrated in every competition. Nevertheless, a company improves its production and service by providing adequate and suitable training to employees. Then the person's own pride of craft takes over.

Deming said that experience without theory teaches nothing. Theory is provided by education and training. I once overheard an argument between two technicians, one of whom was claiming to be correct because he had seventeen years of experience. The other retorted: "You don't have seventeen years of experience. You have one year of experience repeated seventeen times." This is another way of saying that skill is developed through training.

Many companies skimp on training, and a few provide none at all. They hire a given skill level when it's needed, then let it go when it's not. Such companies have high turnover rates and low survival rates because they can't attract and retain skilled employees. They're unable, over the long term, to satisfy their customers. Of course, an adequate skill level doesn't ensure quality, but you can't get there without it. Skill is an ethical issue because it's the basis of an employee's sense of self-worth. It therefore affects the quality of human behavior.

Empowerment

The basis of empowerment is the recognition that trained people are competent in what they do and have a valuable bottom-up view. Building on training and experience, they gain a strong vested interest in doing what they think is necessary to do their jobs. Joseph Juran and Frank Gryna tell us that the number of conformance decisions made each year is huge in most companies.[10] There's no possibility that the supervisory body can become involved in the details of so many decisions. The work must be organized so that employees can make these decisions themselves.

The Department of Defense used Mil-Q-9858A as a quality management standard for more than fifty years, ending its unique authority in 1994. Although this was done in favor of ISO 9001, some things were lost in the translation. Mil-Q-9858A had a strong employee empowerment endorsement that stated, "Personnel who perform quality functions shall have sufficient, well-defined responsibility, authority, and *organizational freedom* to identify and evaluate quality problems and to initiate, recommend, or provide solutions."[11] In government lingo, the phrase "shall have" is a directive, so the statement is a declaration of empowerment.

ISO 9001:1994 was less forceful in its support of employee responsibility. The words sound the same, but upon close reading we find that a company may "define and document" the authority of employees "who need the organizational freedom to (initiate, recommend, or provide solutions…)."[12] Moreover, ISO 9001:2000 drops the issue altogether.[13]

Why is this important? Suppose the company defines and documents a weak authority in the task description. If the documented authority is weak and employees are directed to fudge the numbers, they can't, on the basis of quality, refuse to do so. Moreover, if an auditor finds coercion to be a management tactic, against what clause of the standard is it written to?

Paul Hershey and Kenneth Blanchard described the modes of employee empowerment, tracing them historically.[14] At the low end, they list the *tell* mode, in which management literally tells the employee what to do at each stage of a process. This mode was formalized by Frederick W. Taylor and worked reasonably well in the early part of the 19th century.[15] The *delegate* mode is the high end of empowerment, in which employee responsibility is delegated, and the employee is responsible for quality performance.

Although most companies boast of their employee relationship, the reality on the factory floor may be quite different. Many of us, in the heat of production schedules, have overheard management demand that tests be waived, data be changed, or defects be tolerated. As ISO 9001 now stands, the tell mode is acceptable if it's supported by documentation. Empowerment is an ethical issue because it establishes the authority of employees in the performance of their effort. Therefore, it affects the quality of human decision.

Fear

Deming's point eight, drive out fear, seems somewhat out of place today—archaic and inappropriate to modern quality. In his great wisdom, Deming knew better. He understood that fear is, and continues to be, a management tool. It's manifested in many ways, principally by exhortations to meet production targets and quotas or else find another job. I'm reminded of the threat often used in the textile industry during the 1930s: "If you can't do this job faster, there's a barefoot man out there who can and who wants your job!"[16] The modern words to this melody are, "If you can't get your numbers up, this plant's moving to Mexico!" Carol J. Loomis describes a "tone at the top" at the Lucent Corp. that drove employees to make false production claims.[17] None of this was illegal, so no one went to prison, but the public was misled. Warren Bennis talks about the culture of fear at *The New York Times*, which led to the recent dismissal of two top executives.[18] Says Bennis, "Organizational cultures are not like breaking news stories: They evolve slowly, imperceptibly, over years if not decades."

The elements of fear are coercion, threats, abuse, and disempowerment. It all comes down to fear. Coercion is unacceptable, but unless it's in violation of the penal code, the existing standards of quality aren't well designed to deal with it. Threats and abuse are similarly passed over in the standards, as though their presence is negligible in the modern workplace. The crippling effect of disempowerment is a result of managerial decision; where it exists, management has already decided to disregard the consequences. Fear is an ethical issue because it's a fundamental negative motivator, adverse to human health.

To summarize, the basis of a standard of ethical behavior in business is defined in three notions: skill, empowerment, and absence of fear. Deming's points two and six stress the need for training to increase skill, permitting empowerment. Points seven, nine, and twelve encourage sufficient empowerment of the employees, enabling them to make decisions about their jobs. Points eight and eleven relieve fear, permitting employees to devote their efforts and imagination to their tasks.

A CODE OF ETHICS FOR BUSINESS MANAGEMENT

Profit is the goal, while integrity is the means. To ensure integrity, businesses should adhere to the following standards of ethical conduct:
- Identify customer expectations and use them diligently to achieve customer satisfaction.

- Be honest and open with customers, keeping them informed of progress and pertinent issues during periods of contract performance.
- Assume responsibility for quality, reliability, and safety in products and services. This responsibility will not be delegated.
- Inquire of the customer as to the need for traceability of parts during each period of contract performance. Traceability will be assumed unless absolved by the customer.
- Inform the customer of possible conflicts of interest during a period of contract performance. Respect the confidentiality of customers, employees, and peers.
- Don't discriminate against others—customers, employees, or peers—on the basis of race, religion, or gender.
- Respect the organizational freedom of employees to verify the quality of their work and identify nonconformances. Personnel performing quality functions shall have sufficient, well-defined responsibility and authority to identify and evaluate quality problems, and to initiate, recommend, or provide solutions. No employee will be required to produce defective work.
- Ensure that all reports, certifications, and statements are true and complete.
- Maintain a culture that encourages the ethical conduct of all employees. No employee may be harassed or abused by any other employee. No employee may retaliate or take adverse action against anyone for raising or helping to resolve an issue of integrity. Each employee is encouraged to raise issues of integrity to the level each deems necessary for resolution.

Implementing the Code

Customer satisfaction can't be achieved unless customer expectations are met. Therefore, it's important to get both performer and customer expectations into a contract between the two. Robert Kelley calls this set of expectations the "psychological contract," observing that they're often not communicated and therefore not agreed upon.[19] Unrealized expectations on either side can turn the performer-customer relationship from cooperative to antagonistic. To avoid this outcome, open and frank communication is essential. For example, I recently ordered a new automobile, and after waiting three weeks (while paying for a rental car) it arrived with all the perks I had asked for: stereo sound, CD player, air conditioning, and so on. It also had 250 miles on the odometer. I had the choice of refusing it and waiting three more weeks (while continuing to pay for the rental), or accepting it. It may have been a small thing, but I was considerably disappointed.

What I learned from the experience is that you get what's in the contract and nothing more. And though companies may hasten to adopt a code of ethics, the only way for the customer to ensure that it will be invoked on a particular job is to get it in the contract. The best way to achieve that goal is to include the code in ISO 9001. Then when a contract is awarded to an ISO 9001-registered company, the code comes with it. Violations of the code will be violations of the contract, and the customer can seek redress in civil action.

ISO 9001 isn't designed to detect cheating, coercion, and dissemblance but to detect the random errors made by performers of goodwill. Coercion takes place where there's no goodwill. Covert acts that are legal but discriminate against quality through abuse, coercion, threats, or disempowerment of employees may not be actionable even if detected by ISO 9001 auditors. But if these acts violate terms of the code invoked in a contract, they're actionable in civil law. In this way, management is held accountable to the customer.

Benefits of the Code

Each principle of the code provides a benefit to performers and consumers. Some of the benefits are easy to see, while some require a word or two to clarify them. In order, the special benefits deriving from each principle are:
- Ability to meet customer expectations
- Honesty
- Nondelegable quality
- Traceability, which reduces occasions for waste and fraud
- Respect for privacy and avoidance of conflicts of interest
- Anti-discrimination, which is required by law but inserted in the code for completeness
- Empowerment through organizational freedom, responsibility, and authority
- True reports
- Integrity (the "whistle-blowing" principle, which reduces animosity and punitive action).

The principles, collectively, also provide general benefits to the marketplace as described in the following paragraphs.

Benefits to Management

The code takes ethical policies out of the boardroom and applies them at the process level. ISO 9001 requires a quality policy, which always sounds grand, but quality auditors know that the proof of effective quality policy isn't a grand statement but rather the application of specific policies at the process level: policies on waste, measurement, test and inspection, storage, human resources, and the multitude of value-adding activities throughout the company. For example, QS-9000-

registered Ford Motor Co. must have had a quality policy prior to the Bridgestone/Firestone affair because QS-9000 requires one. Yet, Hoyer reports that in regard to customer needs, Ford's policy was ineffective at the process level.[19]

The code reduces liability and risk of high-damage awards. For example, assume that a company is ISO 9001-registered, attesting to a production system under control. Suppose a plaintiff can show that the company is noncompliant with ISO 9001 and is in nonconformance with accepted measurement procedures. The control of the production system is then unverified, and the producer has no way of knowing whether its products meet requirements. Therefore, the plaintiff is justified in suing for the full value of purchased product.

Whistle-blowing creates a venomous atmosphere in the workplace as the workforce becomes divided between those supporting the company and those supporting the whistle-blower. This animosity can sometimes result in slashed tires, smashed windows, and even physical violence. The code empowers employees to appeal to all levels of management, thus replacing fear with fairness. Ethical policies affect the performance of employees. By ensuring ethical management at the process level, the company enhances process performance and benefits management in return.

Benefits to Employees

Deming often discussed pride of workmanship, believing that a skilled, empowered employee would willingly manifest this pride to the benefit of employee and employer alike. Tom Watson believed the same, preferring employees who identified with their company, wanting to improve their jobs, output, and company. Deming and Watson understood that such employees feel a sense of satisfaction and awareness of their contribution to company, family, and society.

Contrast the contributors with a disgruntled employee who, embittered from frustration, disempowerment, overwork, underachievement, inadequate training, and lack of recognition, fights back. The weapons of the disgruntled are deceit, benign neglect, malicious compliance, and sabotage. I recall auditing a company in which a demoralized receiving inspector assured me that the company had little or no receipt inspection. This kind of response requires more than a cursory understanding of human nature on the part of the auditor, and can lead to a failed audit. In another recent case, a Navy contractor quit her job, but not before she had erased mission-critical data from the hard drive of her employer's computer.

There may be many reasons why an employee is disgruntled, but the code reduces them by ensuring ethical management at the process level. This relieves employees of distracting and unnecessary burdens and allows them to focus on quality, improve their performance and that of the company, enhance profit sharing, and fulfill their professional aspirations.

Benefits to Customers

Armand Feigenbaum says that quality is what the customer says it is.[20] Determining what the customer wants is one of the major requirements of ISO 9001. A company must put great effort into this determination. Yet, having done so, the customer receives nothing until a product is made or a service is provided. Therefore, process effectiveness and efficiency are critical to the producer-customer relationship.

The code eliminates many of the factors that conflict with good employee performance. It lays the groundwork for process effectiveness and efficiency, and their continual improvement. The code thus enhances the occasions for quality, reliability, timeliness of delivery, meeting of expectations, and good value. These are the benefits offered to the customer by the code.

Benefits to Society

Free societies are composed of employers, employees, and consumers, and employment and consumption are a significant part of our lives. Quality, in all its manifestations, is also a significant part of our lives. A sense of well-being on the job and confidence in the future will color the view many have toward other institutions of society: systems of justice, education, media, marketplace, military, and government. Satisfaction and confidence in one encourages satisfaction and confidence in all, as these institutions have a closed-loop effect on our lives. This is what the Japanese mean by saying that quality adds value to customers and to society.

The purpose of the code is to create an environment in which employee performance can flourish, with resultant, continuing improvement in the quality of products and services. Society is composed of consumers and users of these products and services. Thus, the code benefits society.

All responsible institutions utilize a code of conduct or ethics naturally tailored to their business, which is quite often confidential. There's little uniformity, and customers are generally unaware that there's a negative side to the business that's performing for them. Quality can suffer in such an environment, often legally short-changing the customer. Employees suffer equally—that is, if Deming is correct in his belief that they want to do their best. A contract derived from a universal code of ethics can assure customers, employees, and management that integrity is the means to profit.

REFERENCES

1. Goldratt, Eliyahu and Jeff Cox. *The Goal: A Process of Continual Improvement.* New York: North River Press, 1986.
2. Hayes, Robert M. and Steven C. Wheelwright. *Restoring Our Competitive Edge.* New York: John Wiley, 1990.
3. George, Steven. "How to Speak the Language of Senior Management." *Quality Progress,* May 2003, pp. 30–36.
4. Palmes, Paul and Sandford Liebesman. "Quality's Path to the Boardroom." *Quality Progress,* Oct. 2003, pp. 41–43.
5. McMurtry, Kim. "e-Cheating: Combating a 21st Century Challenge." *Technological Horizons in Education Journal,* Nov. 2001. Tustin, CA.
6. Fain, Margaret and Peggy Bates. "Cheating 101: Paper Mills and You." *Teaching Effectiveness Seminar,* March 5, 1999. Coastal Carolina University. www.coastal.edu/library/presentations/papermil.html.
7. Hoyer, R. W. "Why Quality Gets an 'F'." *Quality Progress,* Oct. 2001, pp. 32–36.
8. Deming, W. Edwards. *Out of the Crisis.* Massachusetts Institute of Technology, Center for Advanced Engineering Study, 1986.
9. Drucker, Peter F. *The Frontiers of Management.* Truman Talley, 1986.
10. Juran, Joseph M., and Frank Gryna. *Quality Planning and Analysis.* New York: McGraw-Hill, 1993.
11. *Mil-Q-9858A—Military Specification: Quality Program Requirements,* Department of Defense, Dec. 16, 1963.
12. *ISO 9001: Quality systems—Model for quality assurance in design, development, production, installation and servicing,* International Organization for Standardization, 1994.
13. *ANSI/ISO/ASQ Q9001-2000: Quality management systems—Requirements.* ASQ Quality Press, 2000.
14. Hersey, Paul, and Kenneth Blanchard. *Management of Organizational Behavior.* Prentice Hall, 1982.
15. Taylor, Frederick W. *Shop Management.* Harper, 1919.
16. Barke, Oscar, and Nelson Blake. *Since 1900.* McMillan, 1962.
17. Loomis, Carol J. "The Whistleblower and the CEO." *Fortune,* July 7, 2003, pp. 88–96.
18. Bennis, Warren. "News Analysis: It's the Culture." *Fast Company,* Aug. 2003, pp. 34–35.
19. Hoyer, R. W. "Why Quality Gets an 'F'." *Quality Progress,* Oct. 2001, pp. 32–36.

20. Feigenbaum, Armand V. *Total Quality Control*. New York: McGraw-Hill, 1991.

CHAPTER 3

CONTRACTS, SPECIFICATIONS, AND STANDARDS

In law, a contract is a formal agreement between parties to enter into reciprocal obligations. It's not necessary that a contract be in writing; verbal contracts are equally enforceable. However, this chapter is concerned with written contracts and, in particular, with contracts of performance. That is, one party agrees to pay another party to do something, usually in a certain way and within a specified time. The first party is often called a customer; the second party is the performer.

Naturally, certain conditions are imposed upon the performance. These conditions are called "specifications" because they specify what must be done. Specifications aren't always expressed in numbers, but often it's practical that they be. Numbers help to demonstrate to the performer exactly what must be done, and they demonstrate to the customer that the thing done is exactly what was wanted. Numbers also help to achieve repeatability.

As an example, parents might hire a tutor to educate their children. A schedule and curriculum is agreed upon, and the education begins. The contract can be satisfactorily executed with no numbers assigned at all. However, if numerical grades are assigned to test scores, the family can in some way measure the effectiveness of the education. Similarly, a customer might want a blue dress. No number is involved. But a specific blue can be identified with a number, perhaps a wavelength, which then enables the customer and performer to agree exactly on expectations, and also enables repeatability.

Sometimes a number must be specified. Suppose that a customer wants a fast car. A *fast* car can't be built. The performer must have some idea of what the customer means by "fast," and that requirement is best identified with a number. This simple example demonstrates a condition that occurs more often than not. The customer wants something, and very often that something is expressed qualitatively. The customer wants fresh vegetables, a durable sofa, an efficient washing machine, or an impressive business suit. The performer can provide or manufacture all of these things to many customers. But for both optimum customer satisfaction and repeatability, all of these things must somehow be expressed quantitatively.

In negotiating the contract, the customer is concerned with how well the job will be done. It's cause for concern if the performer has never done the job before. Usually, the customer will want a performer with some experience. This means that the performer has done the job repeated times and has developed a set of procedures to ensure the quality of the task. This repetition implies that a standard way of doing business has been developed. The standard may be in-house, that is, unique to that performer, or it may be a set of general good business practices used by many performers engaged in similar activities.

Good business practices have been codified into standard procedures by a large number of industries and institutions to improve the capability and professionalism of the industry, and to better achieve the expectations of customers. Simply put, it's good business to use good business practices. These practices apply to how things are made and how they're done. Standards in the former case are called "product standards." Many times legal requirements are imposed upon product standards, especially if the product being made is a medicine or drug. Standards that apply to how things are done are called "performance standards." This book is chiefly concerned with certain kinds of performance standards known as management standards.

Some standards are simply common sense. For example, the prongs on electrical appliances in the United States have a rectangular shape. In Europe they're round. Each area has adopted a standard product that meets the requirements of its customers but may meet no other. The practice in recent years has been to create international standards. For example, desktop computers are often produced that can perform anywhere that meets their power-input requirements.

Thus, it's apparent that contracts, specifications, and standards are inseparably entwined. Sometimes, both customers and performers make the mistake of treating these issues as separate entities. This mistake is grave, and will almost always lead to customer disappointment. The contract must accord exactly what the customer wants and what the performer can deliver. Specifications must be correct translations of customer requirements, which isn't easy because quite often the numbers will mean little to the customer. And the performance must be achieved in a way that's acceptable to both customers and industry standards.

WRITING THE CONTRACT

The contract must include all the obligations of the signatory parties in unambiguous terms. You get what's in the contract and nothing more. For example, during the 1980s the U.S. Navy became concerned about the quality of ship repair in private shipyards, which had little experience with repairing fighting ships, and introduced a standard of quality management to be invoked in repair contracts. However, the Navy's low-bid process ensured that the job scope was underestimated and that the number of persons needed to supervise the tasks was understated. In frustration, the team responsible for the standard, myself included, rewrote the document to require that *at least* three managers would be assigned to a ship-repair job. We got what we wished for—exactly three managers—no matter the size of the job. Whether an $8 million dollar or $80 million dollar project, only three people were assigned to manage the work.

Therefore, the written contract must include, in unambiguous terms, all the applicable specifications and standards needed to accomplish the contract to the satisfaction of the customer. The standards provide the legal requirements and the guidelines of good business practices. The specifications accurately describe the customer requirements.

Customer requirements are those needs expressed by the customer that are relative to the desired product or service, its availability date, and required support, if any. The performer must identify requirements that may not have been expressed by the customer, but which are needed to accomplish the contract. It must also identify regulatory and legal requirements. The three activities—identification, review, and communication—can all be achieved in a single-process, comprehensive contract review.

Contract Review

The formal relationship between a customer and a performer begins with a contract. It can't be stressed enough that the contract defines the quality of the job. This is so because a properly written contract, in which the requirements and inherent characteristics of the product or service are expressed, is the very definition of what the customer is going to get. When supported by ongoing reviews with the participation of the customer, the execution of the contract will meet the customer's expectations. Some expectations will be unexpressed and hence not in the contract, but if it becomes apparent that they're not being met, the contract as written becomes inadequate.

Pete Hybert defines contracting in a way that enhances customer satisfaction, which is the dominant trend in today's intense global competition: "Contracting is the process by which customized systems are designed and delivered."[1] This view goes much further than convention dictates. Most people will agree that the contract isn't over until delivery, but Hybert is saying that *contracting* isn't over until delivery. This is a very important distinction because it carries with it the sense of an ongoing process. It goes beyond the conventional idea that contract review is a single event in the beginning of a contract phase. An effective contracting process will track the dynamic customer requirements and expectations during the entire period of performance.

Figure 3.1 depicts the interrelated steps of an effective contracting process. The first step is identifying customer requirements, which usually starts with an initial meeting of customer and performer. At the same time, a notion of customer expectations is established.

In simple cases a single person may represent each faction. For example, a single customer-agent can express exactly the requirements for an off-the-shelf product, and a single performer-agent can take the order. The performer must determine which of its functions is the primary interface agent with the customer. In some companies it's the marketing department, but in others, a customer service department is the main point of contact.

However, if the product were a large system or complex of some sort, or if the service were a major project, then the contracting process would consist of teams, one representing the customer, the other the performer. For example, if Boeing Aircraft Co. were the performer and United Airlines the customer, each side would present a team of experts representing various functions within each corporation. The performer experts would meet with the customer experts to identify requirements and determine whether those needs could be satisfied by company capability.

The performer's team will have members from marketing, sales and service, design, manufacturing, and purchasing. The customer's team will consist of expert users of one or more of the capabilities that the system will provide (e.g., materials requirements planning users, information technology users, maintenance crews, operators, and human resource planners). A customer purchasing a passenger air-

Figure 3.1—An effective contracting process

Alternate capabilities and plans

Initial requirements and subsequent changes

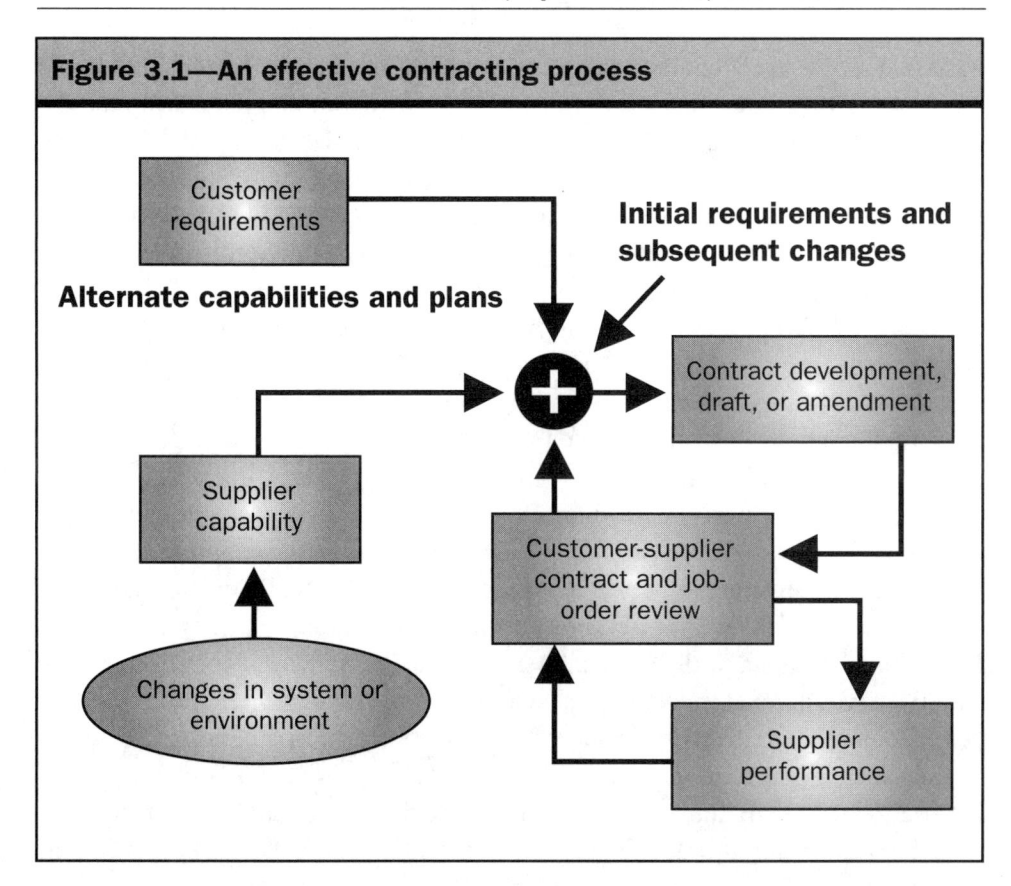

plane will want people in the contract review process who represent its own marketing, service, technical support, and maintenance functions.

Once the customer requirements are identified, the next step is to review the capability of the company to meet the requirements with its existing facilities or to determine if new processes are necessary and feasible. Assuming an initial agreement of expectations between customer and performer, a contract is then developed and an initial review takes place, including the job order if the customer requires it. In some cases, the contract contains the customer requirements and not the specifications. In other cases, the contract will contain both. In all cases the people in operations work from the job order. Thus, even if the customer is able to verify from the contract that the specifications meet the requirements, this doesn't verify the job order, which may contain more, fewer, or different specifications.

The contracting process is structured to maintain an agreement of expectations between the performer and the customer throughout the performance period. This is shown in figure 3.1 as a feedback element of the system. It lets the customer verify that requirements were recorded as they were transmitted and that the specifications are a valid translation of the requirements. During the period of performance, this feedback element provides the customer and performer with an opportunity to review progress and resolve problems together. This helps the customer to understand what must be done, the options available, and their cost. The customer's expectations may rise or fall as a result of the review, which enhances an agreement and satisfaction at the end of the contract.

Figure 3.1 shows that after an agreement on the contract is reached and the company begins the various phases of work—i.e., design, development, and production—periodic contract reviews continue throughout the process. During these reviews, both the customer and the performer may request changes. Perhaps a material is no longer available, or its price has greatly increased, which changes the scope or the cost of the product. Perhaps the customer's requirements have changed. Joint review by customer and performer enhance the opportunities for maintaining an agreement between them of customer expectations. Some of the things that are involved in the contract review process are:

- An initial meeting with the customer is conducted to establish the product or service requirements, including those for delivery and support, if any.
- Customer requirements are balanced against company capabilities and resources, and against regulatory requirements.
- After a contract is drafted, an initial joint review is conducted to ensure that the requirements are adequately defined and confirmed, and specifications documented.
- An ongoing process of periodic contract and performance review takes place in which the customer is a participant, either directly or through continual feedback.
- Customer satisfaction with the final product or service is assessed and recorded.

WRITING SPECIFICATIONS

Specifications can be qualitative, quantitative, or a mix of the two. For example, in U.S. Navy ship repair, the tasks to be done are listed in a work breakdown structure. The entire document, which may contain nearly a thousand tasks, is called the "specification." It specifies in sufficient detail every job that must be done. A schedule is usually associated with the specification and includes the critical path of the effort. The specification is itself a qualitative description of the ship repair, although individual tasks will reference quantitative criteria as necessary.

In design engineering, there are always quantitative criteria that describe critical-to-quality characteristics of the product or service to be manufactured or provided. For example, the design of an engine will include torque criteria. The design of a cafeteria will include queuing time criteria. The criteria usually consist of a target value and tolerances above and below the target value that are relevant to the quality characteristic of the product or service. The tolerances are established in recognition that infinite precision isn't possible. A good deal of thought goes into determining these tolerances, along with recognition that they may have to be changed. For example, the design may specify that a cylinder should be three inches in diameter, ± 0.001 inch, but the engineers may then discover that the production system can't consistently meet these specifications. A certain amount of intuition often goes into specifications. If the production system isn't capable, there are only two choices: widen the specifications or buy a new production system.

Widening the tolerances of the specification increases customer risk. On the other hand, it's expensive to buy new production equipment. A dilemma of this type introduces the notion of ethics and provides one more good reason why the customer should participate in the contract review process. The ability of a performing system, production, or service to meet customer requirements is called "capability." This is formally defined as product variability bounded within specifications. Usually, this means that the product variation is within specification limits. Notice that a process can be stable and not be capable. The variability of the process may well be bounded, but if that variability exceeds the specification, then the process isn't capable. You must design a new process. A process must be stable before its capability can be determined. If the product or service being purchased is quite expensive, the wise customer will ask to see evidence of process stability.

WRITING STANDARDS

Standards provide uniformity in performance. Measurement standards, for example, allow the same measurement to be made of the same parameter, irrespective of conditions, time, or place. Because measurement is always defined in terms of comparison to a standard, there can be no measurement without one. Whether the "measurement" is one of space, weight, management, behavior, virtue, or performance, there must always be a standard of comparison. Notice that the term measurement is used here in its most general sense, from measuring the length of a field to measuring up to one's responsibilities. All measurements must have a standard.

This book is concerned with performance standards. Usually this refers to the performance of management. Figure 3.2 provides a list of a few performance standards that displays the scope of such standards. They cover a wide spectrum of management activity: ethics, information technology (IT), risk, governance, and quality. IT is a special concern because it invariably includes a company's financial system. All of these activities come under the purview of the Sarbanes-Oxley Act

Figure 3.2—Partial list of performance standards and their sponsors

Standard	Sponsor
Principles of Corporate Governance	Organization for Economic Cooperation and Development
OCEG Framework	Open Compliance and Ethics Group
Policy Governance Model	International Policy Governance Association
Enterprise Risk Management Framework	Committee of Sponsoring Organizations of the Treadway Commission
IT Control Objectives for Sarbanes-Oxley	IT Governance Institute
ISO 9001: Quality Management Standard	International Organization for Standardization

of 2002, and certain actions, though once common, are now illegal. Nevertheless, all the sponsors are private organizations. In the free enterprise system, business conduct is regulated by professional or private groups, not by government.

I once attended a national meeting of Navy personnel whose task was to write standard work items. In one effort, negotiations broke down completely over an argument of what "to do" meant. This type of argument is common in anything concerning contracts, and the whole purpose of a standard is to appear in a contract. As a result, wisdom dictates that every standard should begin with definitions of key words that have specific meaning to the standard. Even general words can be given specific meaning for purposes of the contract, but only if the specific definition is provided in the standard. For example, the standard might define "supervise" as: "Lead, oversee, and inspect the work of others."[2] Then, later in the standard, the performer may be required to supervise a given task, and it's clear to customer and performer what must be done from a legal point of view.

It's far better to clarify matters up front than to argue them out before a judge in civil trial. This is why standards should never be written by one person. Drafted, yes; written, no. A team effort during the writing process provides the breadth of view that is likely to be found in the marketplace. On a very large contract, there will be a prime contractor, many subcontractors, and several customers, all interpreting the standard in their own way. If a word or phrase is undefined and has several interpretations, you can bet the contract will get bogged down, and performance will be affected.

A properly written standard will tell the performer *what* to do, but never *how* to do it. There's more at stake than just offending a performer. If you tell the performer how to do the job, you own the result. If things go badly, the performer's plea in civil court will be that he was "just following orders." Sometimes there's a fine line between what and how, requiring a great deal of wisdom and experience in writing contracts and standards. The experience is necessarily of two kinds: experience in the task, so that the difference between what and how is clear to the author, and experience in writing. The writing must be clear and unambiguous, not only to keep performers from being confused but also to keep them from claiming to be confused.

The example used earlier about three-person management teams provides a good demonstration of how a poorly worded standard permits deliberate misunderstanding. We wanted at least three managers, but assumed that if the job required four or five, a greater number would be assigned. However, the contractor took our wording to literally mean that the number three satisfied the requirement of "at least three." And although inadequate, the lesser number was a legal and much cheaper solution.

It's all well and good to talk about meeting customer expectations. Most performers profess to do so, or at least to try. However, business works on profit or the expectation of profit, so rarely do customer and performer have the same expectations. Well-written contracts, specifications, and standards are extremely important in preventing misunderstanding and disappointment of either customer or performer. All too often, abstract notions such as ethics get involved in many contracts. The Sarbanes-Oxley Act is there to help level the playing field.

REFERENCES

1. Hybert, Pete. "Five Ways to Improve the Contracting Process." *Quality Progress*, Feb. 1996, pp. 65–70.
2. *NAVSEA Standard Work Item 009-67*. U.S. Naval Sea Systems Command, June 1989.

CHAPTER 4

QUALITY MANAGEMENT SYSTEMS

One of top management's most important tasks is to ensure the effectiveness and efficiency of the organization's processes. This is a completely general and comprehensive task and applies to all kinds of processes: production, service, government, education, military, commercial, and so on. This task includes defining the management system that will be used to establish and maintain policies, goals, resources, procedures, processes, and effective performance. In short, the task is to define and establish a quality management system (QMS). But before pursuing this idea, it's necessary to discuss a new notion being thrust into the equation—governance.

GOVERNANCE

The field of quality has long focused on systems management as applied to the effectiveness and efficiency of processes. This is as it should be, but it must be recognized that the traditional view, although necessary, is no longer sufficient. The Sarbanes-Oxley Act (SOX) focuses its spotlight on an aspect of management that has become separate from quality—the issue of governance. Although SOX doesn't specifically mention governance, its criteria on management always come down to governance, so with increasing frequency, authorities are raising the issue as fundamental to SOX compliance.

There's no universal definition of governance, but one provided by the Organization for Economic Cooperation and Development (OECD) is finding general acceptance. The Securities and Exchange Commission has accepted it, so it will probably be the eventual winner. Governance is defined as "the system by which business corporations are directed and controlled. The governance structure specifies the distribution of the rights and responsibilities among different participants in the corporation, such as the board, managers, shareholders and other stakeholders, and spells out the rules and procedures for making decisions on corporate affairs. By doing this, it also provides the structure through which the company objectives are set, and the means of attaining those objectives and monitoring performance."[1]

PERFORMANCE STANDARDS

It's stated in chapter 2 that standards applying to how things are done are called performance standards. There's an important ambiguity here. "How" refers to the mechanics of getting things done and implies that the objective is to get them done well. In fact, the two issues are distinct—getting things done isn't the same as getting them done well. For readers with an understanding of statistical quality control, a good analogy is the difference between stability and capability. For example, the well-known and respected Shewhart control charts indicate the stability of a process but say nothing about its capability—how well it works.

So it is with performance standards. One kind of performance standard may be designed to ensure the stability of a QMS; another may be designed to ensure how well the system works. This book will refer to the first kind as a "standard of governance." The reason for this reference should be clear from the definition of governance. Notice that this definition makes no suggestion of how well anything works. The important point in governance is to have a documented and controlled structure whose integrity can be verified under the law.

The second kind will be referred to as a "standard of performance excellence," for obvious reasons. Understanding the dual nature of performance standards and systems, we can return to the traditional notion of a QMS, bearing in mind that this familiar view is only part of the performance requirement. (See figure 4.1.)

QUALITY MANAGEMENT STANDARDS

The term "quality system" is often misunderstood to be concerned with quality assurance or statistical measurements. Although partly true, this

Figure 4.1—System and standard: a symbiotic pair

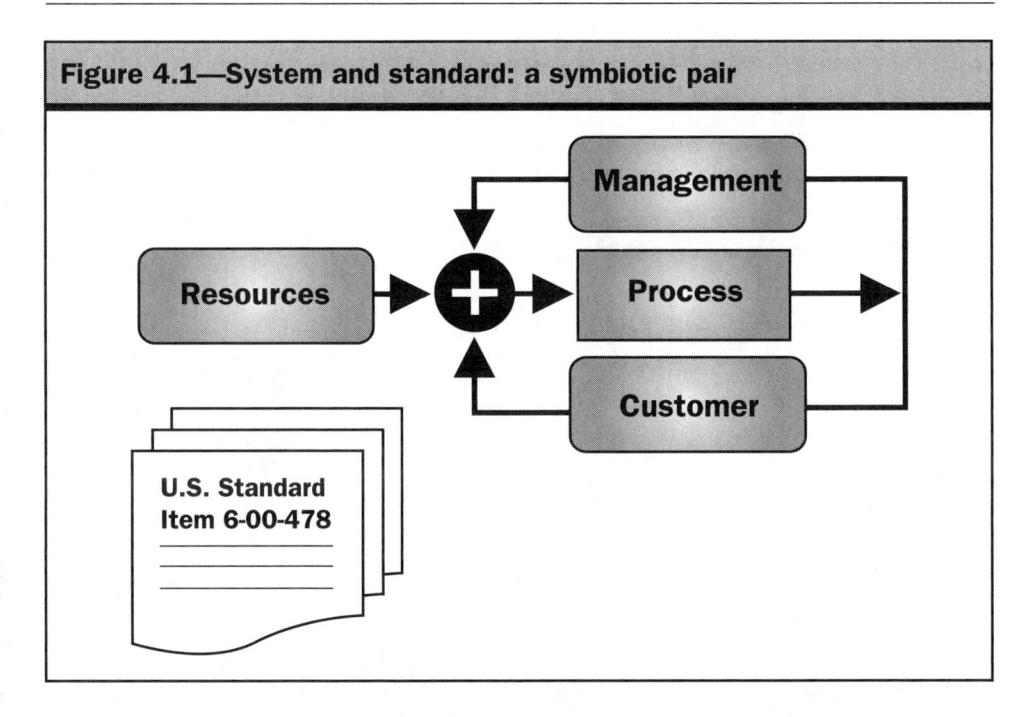

definition is grossly understated. Any system or process in the company that directly or indirectly affects the quality of the company's product or service is a quality system. Therefore, everyone in the company is responsible for quality. And if the company's processes consistently meet or exceed customer expectations in the *goodness* of its products and services, then the company has a *good* quality system.

The quality system should be synergistic and symbiotic—the system output should be greater than the sum of its parts because the parts work together to achieve the synergy. In practical terms, the subsystems are integrated and coordinated to achieve system objectives. All processes that affect the quality of product or service should be organized in the natural flow of things and supported with necessary resources. This type of structure is known as the "process approach" and is suitable to the newer standards of performance. Also, system performance must be continually measured for effectiveness and efficiency, with active improvement structures.

An excellent way to ensure effective and efficient processes is to conform them to good business practices—benchmark processes. Such benchmarks, when widely recognized, become a standard of operation. Thus, standards and systems complement one another in the sense of form and substance. The standard provides the form; the system provides the substance. Although there can be form without substance, there can't be substance without form. In this chapter, we see why this point is important to system design. It means that one simply can't have repeating and systematic performance without a standard operating procedure.

When form and substance both exist, the two are inseparable. Therefore, a discussion on quality management *systems* is begun with a discussion on quality management *standards*—the soul of the system.

Characteristics of a Quality Management Standard

Chapter 3 points out that the first characteristic of a standard is that it provides uniformity in performance. It does this by precise wording aimed at a procedural objective. Notice the focus is on performance *procedure*. There isn't necessarily a requirement for a given level of performance. In this sense, standards are often misunderstood. A standard is, by definition, an agreement among participants to do something in a particular way. If there's little agreement, then there are few participants, and you don't have a standard. Invariably, the standard is a product of compromise because it must appeal to a large group, all volunteers. Purists often criticize a standard if it seems too weak to lead to top performance, but few companies are interested in what someone else might define as top performance. There would be few players if the standard were too tough, so the writers of standards usually employ this strategy: They draft a standard that's acceptable to a given population, then try to toughen it up in ensuing years. Hence, the second characteristic of a standard is that its terms are agreeable to subscribers.

The third characteristic of a standard is that it can stand up in court. Randall Gooden says that for a QMS to protect itself against product liability, it must have a fully documented system of control procedures.[2] This requirement will generally reside in the standard that defines the system. In addition, this same requirement protects the customer in duress and is also a requirement of SOX as it applies to financial controls.[3] It will be shown in later chapters that the law may apply to quality controls as well.

The fourth characteristic of a standard is that it be realizable—blue-sky standards can't be implemented. Every quality system has two parts—the documented part and the physical or implemented part. I assume that the documented part is in compliance with a realizable standard, so for ease in writing about standards and systems, when I refer to a quality system I usually mean the implemented system.

The Quality Toolbox

A "quality system" has been defined as the organizational structure, responsibilities, procedures, processes, and resources for implementing quality management.[4] A "quality management system" has been defined as a system to direct and control an organization with regard to quality.[5] These definitions imply the breadth of education, training, and methodologies necessary to effect the quality of products and services. This "curriculum," for want of a better word, is often called the "quality toolbox." A QMS might use the entire toolbox or only certain tools, so it's worthwhile to take a quick look at just what's in this box.

The academic array in this toolbox would include systems theory, queuing theory, calculus, linear algebra, probability and statistics, logic, and engineering mathematics. The engineering array would include operations research, optimal design, control systems analysis, computer systems, simulation techniques, probability models, reliability, decision analysis, and statistical methods such as design of experiments (DOE), response surfaces, time series analysis, and statistical quality control (SQC). The business array would include project and process management, production and operations, information technology, team dynamics, and resource utilization. It also includes certain Japanese strategies such as the Toyota Production System, *kaizen*, and Taguchi methods. The investigative array would include measurement systems, data collection, sampling, hypothesis testing, capability analysis, problem solving, and auditing.

This list is imposing—as it should be. The gross domestic product (GDP) is the broadest measure of the health of the U.S. economy. It's defined as the output of those goods and services produced by labor and property located in the United States. At the end of 2005, the U.S. GDP was $12.5 trillion.[6] Refer back to chapter 1, under a philosophy for business ethics. The section discussed how the resources of the United States belong to the people. The price tag on those resources is $12.5 trillion. It's an indescribably large management problem that requires much wisdom to manage. The quality toolbox is no small part of the management solution. Armed with this understanding, a few popular quality management systems should be examined to determine if any of them can serve as a standard of governance.

Robust Quality Management Systems

In the technical world, the term "robust" has a somewhat different meaning than when it's generally used. For example, a statistical process that converges to a normal distribution is robust. An algorithmic process that converges to an optimal value is robust. An industrial process that converges to a target value is robust. A robust QMS is one designed to converge to solutions. Some quality methodologies are broad enough in their scope that they're akin to quality management systems. Four of the most prominent are the Malcolm Baldrige program, total quality management (TQM), Six Sigma, and lean.

Malcolm Baldrige National Quality Award

The U.S. Congress established the Malcolm Baldrige National Quality Award (MBNQA) program in 1987, with public law 100-107. The purpose of the program is to establish the global leadership of U.S. industry through continuous improvement of quality methods in product and process. Although the MBNQA criteria are comprehensive, they're periodically updated. In 2005 the criteria covered the following categories: leadership; strategic planning; customer and market focus; human resource focus; measurement, analysis, and knowledge management; process management; and business results.[7] The quality toolbox contains techniques and solutions to help meet the criteria of each of these categories. An applicant company is free to meet the criteria in any way it chooses, and the annual award goes to the best competitors in five groups: manufacturing, small business, service, health care, and education.

The U.S. government has maintained its support and interest in this program, to the point where the president of the United States may preside over the award ceremony. This visibility, and the effectiveness imposed by its criteria, have given enormous prestige to the MBNQA program, and many quality gurus advocate using the program as a quality standard. There's a certain ambiguity in this goal, though. An MBNQA program is clearly a QMS model, and a very good one at that. However, it's an award, not a standard. The criteria are strict and only the most determined and dedicated companies will put the required effort into going after the award. It's not likely that the average company would pursue MBNQA certification any more intensely than it would the award. Remember, if standards are too tough, you have few players. Without offering a certifiable standard, the program would have no legal legs.

Even discounting its capacity as a standard, an MBNQA program has much to offer. It can be used as a freelance model—one in which any amount can be used, wherever desired. In this sense, the program can become a formal QMS of arbitrary design, using a model adapted from the criteria. Piggybacked onto a standard of governance, the system would easily achieve performance excellence.

Total Quality Management

TQM is widely used, but the way it's implemented varies from user to user. It's a freelance system with some common principles. Each user selects the techniques and structure from the quality toolbox that it deems is most suitable to itself. Bohden Oppenheim and Zbigniew Przasnyski offer a comprehensive view of an effective TQM.[8] They conclude that training in the philosophy of quality is required, and advocate using design of experiments and SQC, as well as other useful techniques in problem prevention and correction. The authors call for supervisory training in W. Edwards Deming's maxims, organization, customer satisfaction, leadership, and continual improvement.

TQM can be a comprehensive and effective quality system. As a model, it presents some of the same problems the MBNQA does as a system model. It has no formal sponsor. There's no one to say yes or no as to whether a given TQM system meets a TQM standard, because there is no TQM standard.

Why is it important to have a standards sponsor? Why can't a company simply adopt a formal QMS along the lines of, say, TQM or MBNQA, and let it go at that? The answer is, it can. But the customer risk is high. In a case of great dissatisfaction, a customer couldn't take a performer to court because of noncompliance to an uncertified system. In this sense, a freelance QMS is not customer-sensitive. TQM practitioners will object to this statement because it's such a negative view of a company's sincere attempt to produce quality. This may be true, and in any case it will be the company's claim. However, if the business world were full of good intentions, there would be no need for a law such as SOX. The bottom line of customer satisfaction is always with respect to civil action. TQM has no legal legs, and so it fails one of the characteristics required for a quality management standard.

Six Sigma

Six Sigma is a strategic quality goal and a management methodology.[9] Roger W. Hoerl writes that it is "one of the few technically oriented initiatives to generate significant interest from business leaders, the financial community, and the popular media."[10] This interest is owed, no doubt, to its focus on the corporate bottom line.

The name "Six Sigma" is a statistical term that measures how far a given process deviates from perfection. In this sense, it is akin to the "zero defects" philosophy espoused by Philip Crosby many years ago. The main idea is that the first step to achieving perfection is to measure how many defects there are in a process. Knowing the size of the problem makes it possible to systematically eliminate it.

The objective of a Six Sigma program is to implement a measurement-based strategy that focuses on process improvement and variation reduction, using statistical techniques applied to improvement projects. Thus, Six Sigma is project-oriented. The program is formal in the sense that it employs defined algorithms for design and problem solving. It's also formal in its organizational structure.

34 **ISO 9001 and Sarbanes-Oxley**: A System of Governance

The Six Sigma structure is hierarchical, as is the structure of most corporations, so the two superimpose quite well. The chief executive officer (CEO) is at the top; then in descending order there's the Quality Leader, Master Black Belts, Process Owners, Black Belts, and Green Belts. This structure is integrated with the company organization perfectly. The Quality Leader reports directly to the CEO; there is, in principle, a Master Black Belt for each major function of the company; the process owners are exactly as their name implies—the chief *doers* of the company, and on down to full-time and part-time project managers. The genius of it all is the Six Sigma recognition that process owners must be integrated into the system. Thus, the very heart of the company buys into Six Sigma because they're a part of it. The old-style quality assurance structure was rarely able to achieve this necessary integration.

There are a few caveats to a Six Sigma program that aren't necessarily shortcomings but can easily degenerate to such. The first is the fundamental nature of project orientation. Project thinking brings both strengths and weaknesses. The strength is obvious: Each process in the company can address problems one after another, always moving toward improvement and always recording financial gains because the program requires reporting on financial goals. The downside is that Six Sigma is a great de-optimizer. As Eliyahu Goldratt explains it, a system has both subsystem and total system constraints, and they're usually not the same.[11] Therefore, if each subsystem attempts to optimize itself, the total system will be suboptimal.

Philosophically, project orientation is the opposite of strategic orientation. Both are necessary to long-term success, but there's little that's inherent in Six Sigma to address the big picture. The success of Six Sigma requires its techniques to be integrated with a company's existing strategic and visionary structure. Fundamentally, it's a problem-solving methodology.

Six Sigma is also thought to be very expensive to implement, so much so that a 2003 survey reports 90 percent of Six Sigma users were units or divisions of large corporations.[12] The same survey reports that 98 percent of U.S. corporations are small businesses. Not long ago, it could cost up to $20,000 to train a Master Black Belt. The cost of Black Belt training was rarely below $3,000–$5,000, plus the six-week (or more) loss of the employee while in training. When you combine these costs with the inevitable diminishing returns of pursuing perfection, it explains why the survey shows so few companies using Six Sigma and why more than 80 percent have ceased using it after four or five years.

Nevertheless, one Six Sigma executive vice president finds that a Six Sigma program remains very effective at solving major and difficult problems and should never be discarded, once installed. In his own company, the program is used to solve major problems and remains integrated with a strategic system. It's not used as a QMS.[13]

The last caveat is particularly relevant to the purpose of this book. Companies don't get certified in Six Sigma—individuals do. And there's no single certifying authority, although the American Society for Quality is moving in that direction. ASQ has created a body of knowledge for Black Belts and conducts a certification program. However, so do many independent operators, and as long as the business is so lucrative, it will be difficult to centralize this authority. Many companies, resisting the high cost of training, may pay for the certification of one employee, and then train the remaining team in-house. This is freelance certification.

Therefore, as effective and efficient as Six Sigma is as a quality methodology, it can't serve as a QMS standard in a legal sense. The Six Sigma measuring stick for effectiveness isn't structure, but goal achievement, and is determined by money.

How would a company be certified in Six Sigma? By how much money it saved? By the success rate of its goal achievement? I once worked for a company that measured itself by the number of job orders it closed in one year. If at the end of the year the numbers didn't look good, the employees were set to work to expand completed job orders. For example, if a job order had been to replace ten tarpaulin snaps, then that job order was replaced by ten job orders, one for each snap. Needless to say, our goal achievement was always outstanding, whether we had a good year or not. This splendid performance could be achieved in an afternoon.

Six Sigma lacks the first three of the necessary QMS characteristics, although it could meet the fourth easily enough. Similar comments that I made about MBNQA apply here: A Six Sigma program can be used as a freelance model—you use as much of it as you want, where you want, when you want. You get the power of Six Sigma to solve problems and gain improvements, and you can superimpose this capability on any formal QMS.

Lean

Once the aversion to using "lean" as a noun is overcome, it's found to be an efficient manufacturing process. Lean is a derivative of the Toyota Production System.[14] It focuses on pull production, continuous flow, and on waste and cost reduction through both incremental and breakthrough improvements. To get a flavor of lean, consider that one of the important measures of lean effectiveness is "touch time," the amount of time a product is actually being worked on.

In keeping with its Japanese origins, Drew Lathin and Ron Mitchell claim that lean works best in those companies where there are good social relationships.[15]

The authors define two systems that must be integrated in a company: the technical system and the social system. The first includes the company's technology and work processes. The latter includes the people, the organizational structure, and the culture. Of course, any company would benefit by the integration of these two systems, but the integration is an absolute requirement for lean, given its focus on reducing cost and waste through constant employee observation and cooperation.

A study by David Nave compares the improvement programs of lean and of Six Sigma, and his comments are particularly useful in evaluating these methodologies as quality management systems.[16] For example, the author states as a Six Sigma shortcoming that system interaction isn't considered, and that processes are improved independently. This comment reinforces my earlier statement that Six Sigma is a de-optimizer. Nave then gives as a lean shortcoming that the method isn't strong on statistical or system analysis. Put together, the comments raise questions on the effectiveness of either method as a grand management system.

Robert Green offers a different conclusion, describing a QMS that's composed of lean, plus a structure called "J4000," from the Society of Automotive Engineers.[17] J4000 is a standard of best practices in management, human resources, supplier integration, and process flow. In short, the issue of lean as a QMS is finessed; the author describes a case where it's piggybacked onto a standard and provides a capability in both governance and performance excellence.

Performance Standards Versus Control Standards

In a competitive global economy, there's a need for a performance standard that can deliver top performance in terms of effectiveness and efficiency of process, quality of product, and profits. The latter can't be overestimated. In the book *The Goal,* Eliyahu M. Goldratt and Jeff Cox assert that the goal of a (manufacturing) company is to make money.[18] This objective is so powerful that it suggests a serious shortcoming in Six Sigma, which measures project success in terms of financial gain. This metric is less effective than meets the eye because there are a lot of ways in which you can improve a process to increase profits, without doing anything at all for quality. The improvement in financial return may even adversely affect quality. Who makes the decision? It will be the CEO, not the quality leader.

On the other hand, in a litigious economy there's a need for a performance standard that contains sufficient documented controls to establish innocence or culpability in court. Therefore, standards of governance and standards of performance excellence are almost mutually exclusive. The controls required by the former are usually not value-adding steps, and so would be rejected by the latter. Therefore, no single standard can be written to wed the two sets of requirements.

However, a QMS can be built from two different standards, say a standard for performance excellence and a standard for governance. Pete Robustelli and Robert Green independently describe such a hybrid system in their papers referenced earlier.

Addendum

The term "freelance" is used several times in this chapter without being defined. While reading through the chapter, self-assessment and benchmarking may have come to mind at its mention, so I'd like to define all of the terms in this way: "Freelance" means to create your own system. "Self-assessment" means to refer to, or "benchmark" to a standard or a well-defined system, and then declare your own system compliant with the model. In principle, there's nothing wrong with either strategy. The problem comes with being completely honest with yourself in deciding whether you really are compliant. Self-criticism is difficult.

REFERENCES

1. Organization for Economic Cooperation and Development. *OECD Principles of Corporate Governance.* OECD Publications Service, 2004.
2. Gooden, Randall. "How a Good Quality Management System Can Limit Lawsuits." *Quality Progress,* June 2001, pp. 55–59.
3. H. R. 3763, The Sarbanes-Oxley Act of 2002. 107th Congress of the United States of America, Washington, DC, Jan. 23, 2002.
4. ANSI/ISO/ASQC Q10011-1-1994. *American National Standard: Guidelines for Auditing Quality Systems.* American Society for Quality, 1994.
5. ANSI/ISO/ASQ Q9000-2000. *American National Standard: Quality Management Systems—Fundamentals and Vocabulary.* American Society for Quality, 2000.
6. *Gross Domestic Product of the United States.* Bureau of Economic Analysis of the U.S. Department of Commerce, 2005.
7. *Criteria for Performance Excellence.* Baldrige National Quality Program, 2005.
8. Oppenheim, Bohdan, and Zbigniew Przasnyski. "Total Quality Requires Serious Training." *Quality Progress,* Oct. 1999, pp. 63–73.
9. *Six Sigma Quality.* GE Fanuc brochure, GE Co., 1998.
10. Hoerl, Roger. "Six Sigma Black Belts: What Do They Need to Know?" *Journal of Quality Technology,* American Society for Quality, Oct. 2001, pp. 391–406.

11. Goldratt, Eliyahu. *What Is This Thing Called Theory of Constraints and How Can It Be Implemented?* New York: North River Press, 1990.
12. Dusharme, Dirk. "Six Sigma Survey." *Quality Digest,* Feb. 2003, pp. 24–32.
13. Robustelli, Pete. "Beyond Six Sigma." *Quality Digest,* Sept. 2003, pp. 24–28.
14. Liker, J. K. *The Toyota Way.* New York: McGraw-Hill, 2004.
15. Lathin, Drew, and Ron Mitchell. "Learning from Mistakes." *Quality Progress,* June 2001, pp. 39–45.
16. Nave, David. "How to Compare Six Sigma, Lean, and the Theory of Constraints." *Quality Progress,* Mar. 2002, pp. 73–78.
17. Green, Robert. "Bare Bones Production." *Quality Digest,* Feb. 2002, pp. 23–27.
18. Goldratt, Eliyahu M., and Jeff Cox. *The Goal: A Process of Continuous Improvement.* New York: North River Press, 1986.

CHAPTER 5

ISO 9000 QUALITY MANAGEMENT SYSTEM

"*ISO 9001-certified!*" There have been few declarations both so honored and scorned as this one. Across the nation, blue banners can be found stretched out across the porticos of business after business, proclaiming their certification. Also found across the nation are numerous articles in technical journals, denouncing the standard as an expensive and impotent quality charade. This chapter gets at the truth of the matter, beginning with a little history about quality standards.

BACKGROUND ON QUALITY STANDARDS

Formal work standards have been with us for centuries, since the Middle Ages at least. European craft guilds of the 11th to 15th centuries developed and maintained high standards of finished work. This quality was seen in furniture, cathedrals, and châteaux, and we still marvel at the results. The craftsmen were divided into three categories: master, journeyman, and apprentice, and the quality of one's work had to be demonstrated to gain admission to the guild. Within a shop, the quality of the product was inspected by the master. Mohammed Hashim and Mujeeb Khan relate that these ideas are indicated by the Guild Act of 11th century England, whereby representatives of the king were invested with the power to enforce uniformity in "places of manufacture where the wardens of the crafts were appointed to see the work to be good and right and to reform what defects they should find therein, and thereupon inflict due punishment upon offenders and to stamp only good work with the seal of approval."[1]

The practice of ensuring the quality of a product by inspection, using a product standard as a reference, is still widely used today. For example, many manufacturers routinely use a sampled inspection scheme called acceptance testing to verify the quality of incoming material and finished product. As another example, the U.S. Navy uses a very extensive inspection program to verify the repair of its ships in shipyards across the country.

Product inspection has certain limitations. The first is obvious: A defect found in a final product or delivered service is after the fact—it has already occurred. Ideally, it would be better to prevent the defective occurrence in the first place. To shift the emphasis from correction to prevention, one must address the processes that created the product or service.

The second limitation on the inspection/correction philosophy lies in the sheer magnitude of modern producing and servicing enterprises. Large-scale production and service activities today require not only large numbers of direct processes, but large numbers of support processes, as well. It makes sense that all of them function in some synergistic way to ensure product and service quality.

GENESIS OF ISO 9000

The ancestry of ISO 9000 begins with World War II. Coalitions on both sides of the war required some means of uniformity of product. Production levels attained historically unimaginable heights, but there was no way product quality could be ensured using traditional product standards. Yet, the result of poor product quality could've been grave. Mass production of bullets with too little powder, shells with too much, or cannon barrels with fault fractures could've led to unrecoverable losses in the age of blitzkrieg.

Wartime research brought advances in probability theory, statistical techniques, systems analysis, and operations research that could be applied to production methods. In particular, this led to developments in process quality methods, as opposed to those of product quality. The basis of process quality is the notion that if the process is good, the product will be good, too, even in mass production. Some of this research, such as that of Walter Shewhart, had been done prior to the war but gained major impetus in wartime demands.[2]

Therefore, World War II brought about the development of quality systems, which were composed of an inspection scheme augmented by a program of quality assurance (QA) that acted *ex parte* over business operations. A classic example of this kind of system, used for more than fifty years throughout the defense industry, was defined by the standards Mil-Q-45208 and Mil-Q-9858, which pertained to inspection systems and QA systems, respectively. Those familiar with ISO 9001 can find similarities in Mil-Q-9858, which required procedures for contract review, documentation control, and manufacturing control.

After the war, the world's economy began to slowly unify to a single marketplace. In 1947, the General Agreement on Tariffs and Trade (GATT) was signed, which defined standards of trade, production, and service. In accord with this trend, the European Economic Community was created in 1979, one in a series of free trade groups culminating in today's European Union. An important idea in this transition was that uniformity could be achieved through common standards and that this uniformity was necessary. Also, quality standards were seen as a mechanism for leveling the competitive field. In 1946, the International Organization for Standardization (ISO) was established in Switzerland and assumed responsibility for the oversight of standards of various member nations. One of its most utilized standards was ISO 9000, Quality Management Systems—Requirements, first issued in 1987. Arguably, the antecedent of Mil-Q-9858A is also the antecedent of ISO 9000. So although the ISO standards are published in Europe, their procedures are agreed upon internationally.

ISO 9000 IN THE UNITED STATES

During the 1970s, Japanese electronic and automobile manufacturers began to achieve deep inroads in the American market, and U.S. manufacturers were obliged to recognize that the economy was global. Despite strategies such as import quotas and appeals to patriotism, Americans were showing an increasing willingness to purchase foreign products if they believed that those products had superior quality. Many companies adopted ISO 9000 as their standard for a quality management system (QMS). Those companies with an interest in exporting their products had little choice because ISO 9000 certification became a market requirement in most industrial nations.

In the United States, administration of the ISO 9000 QMS program is assumed by the American National Standards Institute (ANSI) and the American Society for Quality (ASQ), which jointly accredits the program through the ANSI-ASQ National Accreditation Board (ANAB). The ANAB accredits private companies as certification bodies, or registrars, which are then authorized to certify manufacturers and providers of service to ISO 9001. Some certified companies are government agencies, such as the Naval Surface Warfare Center in Carderock, Maryland. Total certification in the United States today is estimated at about 40,000 companies.[3]

ISO 9001 certification remains underrepresented in the United States, even at 40,000. Much of the opposition stems from its requirement for documentation and controls, and its lack of requirement for performance excellence. And Americans, who are demonstrably a litigious people, have been naive about the need for controls. For example, one respected author wrote a few years ago that quality controls had seen their day and were actually impeding progress.[4] That may well be true, but progress isn't the reason for controls, litigation is.

STRUCTURE OF ISO 9000:2000

ISO 9000 was drastically restructured in the year 2000 to improve its adaptability to the way modern businesses are organized. Its format uses a process approach, which is an important system characteristic that will be commented on in some detail in this chapter.

The term "ISO 9000" is somewhat ambiguous. It's properly used in two ways. First, ISO 9000 is a *series* of standards for quality management systems, and second, it's the first standard in the set, which includes:

- ISO 9000: Quality management systems—Fundamentals and vocabulary
- ISO 9001: Quality management systems—Requirements
- ISO 9004: Quality management systems—Guidelines for performance improvement

Although certification to ISO 9001 is formal, a company is free to forego certification and simply use it as a model, implementing it as it sees fit. This is called either self-assessment or benchmarking and carries no recognition beyond the company. Most organizations choose to obtain certification, granted by certifying bodies operating under the auspices of the ANAB.

As their titles imply, ISO 9000 and ISO 9004 are advisory. Only ISO 9001 has contractual requirements, which could be the reason why many companies shortsightedly implement just this single part of the standard, more or less ignoring ISO 9004.

ISO 9001 is the focus of discussion, partly because of its contractual terms, but mostly because of its descriptions of governance. This book is about ISO 9000, the Sarbanes-Oxley Act, and the intersection of the law and the standard. Because this intersection occurs at the level of governance, SOX is chiefly applicable to ISO 9001.

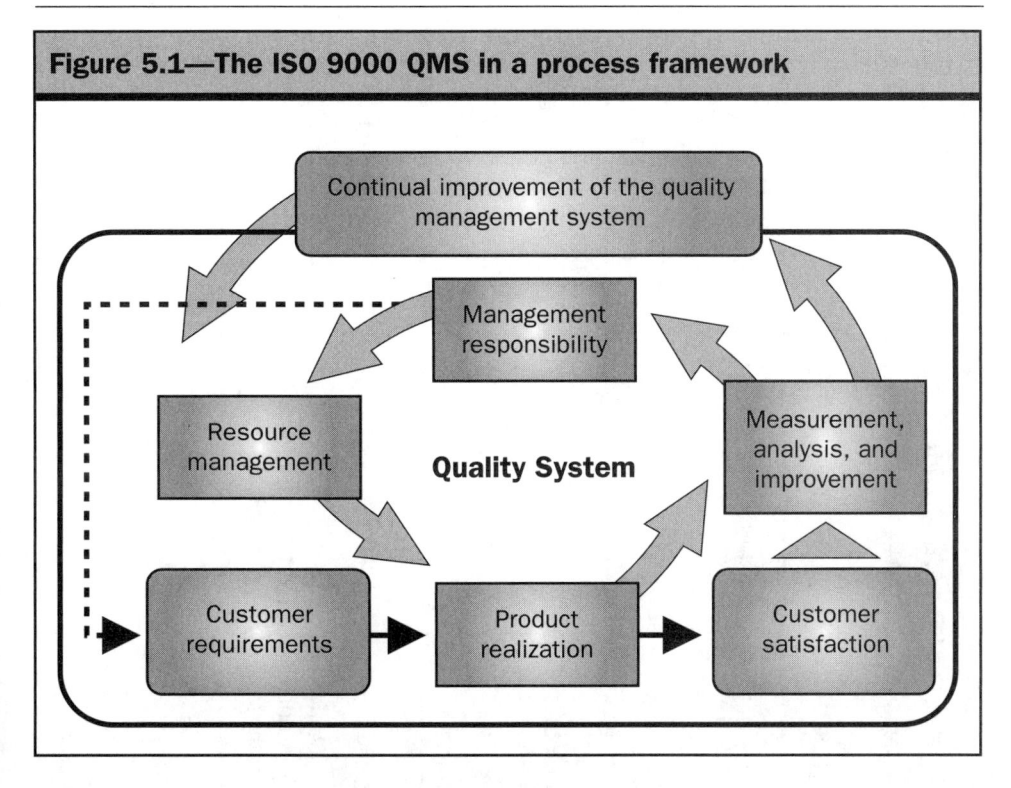

Figure 5.1—The ISO 9000 QMS in a process framework

[Diagram showing: Continual improvement of the quality management system encompassing Management responsibility, Resource management, Measurement, analysis, and improvement within the Quality System; with flow from Customer requirements → Product realization → Customer satisfaction]

ISO 9001: A PROCESS APPROACH

ISO 9001 is structured in a process approach with four core requirements configured as processes within a QMS, as depicted in figure 5.1. The requirements in this flowchart are numbered by clause in the standard. They are:

- Clause 5: Management responsibility
- Clause 6: Resource management
- Clause 7: Product realization
- Clause 8: Measurement, analysis, and improvement

From a systems perspective they're all subsystems of the quality system, which has general requirements described under clause 4.

The requirements are expressed in terms of top management and pertain to those processes that may affect quality. The title of one of them, "Product realization," is perhaps an unfortunate term because it seems to preclude service industries. Nevertheless, ISO 9001 is adaptable to service, and operations processes are adequately described under clause 7. In application, these top-level requirements of ISO 9001 are necessarily approached at a more detailed level. Figure 5.2 provides a breakdown of these core requirements in terms of specific responsibilities whose accomplishment can be measured.

Figure 5.2—Quality management system requirements of ISO 9001/9004:2000

4.0 Quality management system	5.0 Management responsibility	6.0 Resource management	7.0 Product realization	8.0 Measurement, analysis, and improvement
4.1 General	5.1 Management commitment	6.1 Provision	7.1 Planning	8.1 General
4.2 Documentation	5.2 Customer focus	6.2 Human resources	7.2 Customer-related processes	8.2 Monitoring and measuring
4.3 Quality management principles	5.3 Quality policy	6.3 Infrastructure	7.3 Design and development	8.3 Control of nonconforming product
	5.4 Planning	6.4 Work environment	7.4 Purchasing	8.4 Data analysis
	5.5 Responsibility, authority, communication	6.5 Information	7.5 Production and service provision	8.5 Improvement
	5.6 Management review	6.6 Suppliers and partnerships	7.6 Control of measuring devices	
		6.7 Natural resources		
		6.8 Financial resources		

Fundamentally, ISO 9001 requires that the factors governing quality of product be under control, and that the process be documented. The details of implementation are left to individual companies on the grounds that each company has its own way of doing business. The scope of ISO 9000 is defined by its requirements that are applicable to a particular company, and so depends upon the breadth of that company's operations. For example, a company that provides no service or does no design will have less breadth of operation than one that does, and will have fewer ISO 9001 requirements upon it. This flexibility is known as exclusion. Processes that are defined in ISO 9001 but which don't exist in the company, or that do exist but will have no affect on customer satisfaction with the product or service, are excused from compliance.

From the legal point of view, documentation is a major asset of ISO 9001 because it provides records and internal controls. You have a cycle of paperwork in every business transaction: sales orders, purchase orders, job orders, and delivery orders. Figure 5.3 shows this cycle as it might apply to manufacturing. Various records are used in this cycle for customer requirements, design, specifications, parts and materials, fabrication and assembly, test and inspec-

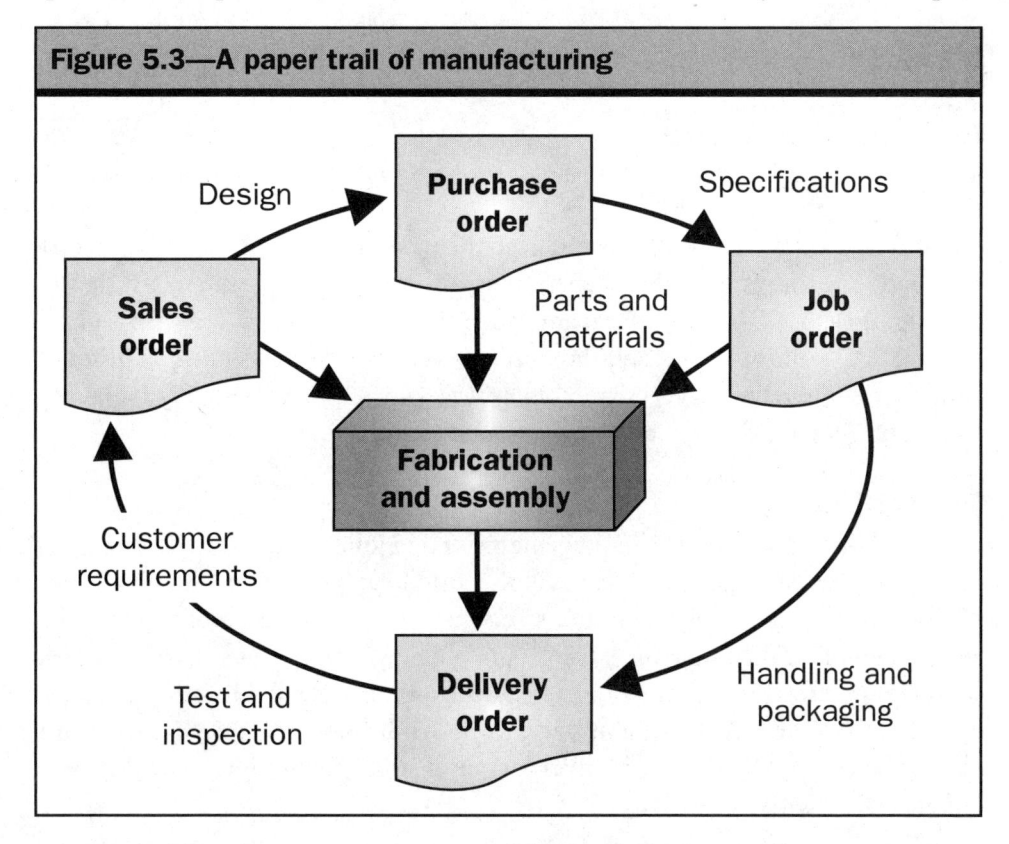

Figure 5.3—A paper trail of manufacturing

tion, and handling and packaging. This documentation defines a paper trail from customer expectations to delivery. If customer dissatisfaction leads to litigation, the law will become very interested in this paper trail from the perspective of records and controls.

Creating a partial list of the documentation in a paper trail of business is worth considering. It can highlight the issues that might seem bureaucratic to the efficiency expert but absolutely necessary to the investigator. The list includes:

- Authorizations
- Change orders
- Contracts
- Criteria and tolerances
- Delivery orders
- Dispositions
- Job orders
- Measurements
- Policies
- Procedures
- Purchase orders
- Retention
- Signatures
- Test and inspection results
- Traceability

Following the collapse of customer confidence in the aftermath of the 2001 corporation scandals, the U.S. Department of Justice became very interested in paper trails and controls. A company can get in trouble if the trail isn't clear. Under SOX, both evidence and the absence of evidence may work against the wrongdoer. In the past, a company might have to pay a fine for wrongdoing, but under SOX, the CEO could also go to prison.

GE FANUC

GE Fanuc Automation is a global enterprise and joint venture of General Electric Co. and FANUC LTD of Japan.[5] With world headquarters in Charlottesville, Virginia, the company has operations serving the Americas, Europe, and Asia, with a total of 1,500 employees. GE Fanuc provides both products and services, specializing in factory automation. This dedication is reflected in the company's mission statement: "At GE Fanuc, we work toward a single goal: To improve our customers' productivity with the best automation technology, reliability, and services worldwide."

The company provides consulting, design, and support services across a wide spectrum of industries and in diverse applications, from machining systems in large aerospace applications, to process control systems in wastewater plants, to software tools and hardware components used by original equipment manufacturers worldwide. GE Fanuc not only provides consulting services in planning appropriate processes and systems for client requirements, but also manages the installation of the network infrastructure, through the software device level. This installation is further enhanced by training and full-service support.

GE Fanuc is certified to ISO 9001:2000 and is registered with the British Standards Institute. In keeping with the GE Corp. family, GE Fanuc has an extensive Six Sigma quality initiative, managed by the vice president for information technology, who is also the Quality Leader. The company has three master Black Belts, four full-time Black Belts, and 20–30 functional Black Belts—employees who serve in various positions but who have certified as Black Belts and are able to use their quality techniques in their jobs. GE Fanuc considers it desirable and normal for its employees to be trained in statistical methods, whatever their job description. This is true quality function deployment.

Tina Kennealy, the ISO management representative, reports to the vice president of manufacturing and regards the ISO 9001 structure as the mechanism that "keeps us on track and not too far from where we ought to be."[6] She reports all costs of quality in terms of dollars and units of production to top management. This provides an executive-level assessment of the material costs of its quality as well as an accurate picture of unit cost for its diversity of products.

GE Fanuc fits in quite well with the picture advocated in this book—maintaining a system of governance that's provided by ISO 9000 and a system of performance excellence provided by its Black Belt quality initiative. Moreover, the organization's costs of quality reports to top management put it ahead of the pack in anticipation of the day when SOX extends to operations. This case study shows the feasibility of using the two kinds of systems synergistically.

Still, we see here the residual effect of quality's long association with manufacturing. Whereas the Six Sigma quality initiative is conducted companywide, the benefits of ISO 9000 as a system of governance are largely restricted to the manufacturing function.

A FINAL WORD

In the section on the structure of ISO 9000:2000, I commented that ISO 9000 and ISO 9004 are advisory only. Because ISO 9001 has contractual requirements, many companies implement only ISO 9001 and more or less ignore ISO 9004. This shortsightedness is at the heart of the criticism—strong on form and weak on substance. In other words, the weakness is not because of ISO 9000, but because of the weak way in which it's frequently implemented.

According to Jack West, former chairman of the U.S. Technical Advisory Group 176 and lead U.S. delegate to ISO Technical Committee 176, an enterprise needs both ISO 9001 and ISO 9004. The first standard provides governance, the *form* of ISO 9000. ISO 9004 provides a performance excellence model that can make a company a world-class competitor. This is the *substance* of ISO 9000. West calls ISO 9001 and ISO 9004 a "consistent pair" that will enhance market success.[7] Thus, ISO 9000 is both a standard of governance and, if fully implemented, a standard of performance excellence equal to any other.

REFERENCES

1. Hashim, Mohammad, and Mujeeb Khan. "Quality Standards: Past, Present, and Future." *Quality Progress*, June 1990, pp. 56–59.
2. Shewhart, Walter A. *Economic Control of Quality of Manufactured Product*. Princeton, New Jersey: Van Nostrand, 1931.
3. Corbett, Charles. "The Financial Impact of ISO 9000 Certification in the U.S." *UCLA Anderson School of Management,* July 2004.
4. Pyzdek, Thomas. "Quality Profession Must Learn to Heed Its Own Advice." *Quality Progress,* June 1999, pp. 60–64.
5. GE Fanuc Automation. *www.gefanuc.com.* General Electric Co., 2005.
6. GE Fanuc. Conversation with Tina Kennealy, product quality Black Belt and ISO 9000 management representative. Charlottesville, Virginia, Feb. 16, 2005.
7. West, J., J. Tsiakais, and C. Cianfrani. "Standards Outlook: The Big Picture." *Quality Progress,* Jan. 2000, pp. 106–110.

CHAPTER 6

SARBANES-OXLEY

The Enron Corp. of Houston, Texas, filed for bankruptcy in December 2001, after having admitted to inflated earnings of nearly $600 million. With $62.8 billion in assets, it became the largest bankruptcy case in U.S. history.[1] It also became, for many, a symbol of corporate greed and management dishonesty. Unfortunately, Enron wasn't alone. WorldCom, Qwest, Tyco, Adelphia, Global Crossing, Lucent, ImClone, and Arthur Andersen are just a few of the dozens of U.S. corporations that came under scrutiny by the Justice Department following the Enron scandal. Writer Joseph Nocera of *Fortune* magazine stated that the scandals created a crisis of investor confidence the likes of which hasn't been seen since the Great Depression.[2]

The malfeasance was of two inseparable kinds: fraud and dishonest accounting. The fraud was in the difference between the true value and the paper value of corporate assets. The dishonest accounting had to do with declared value, both to the Internal Revenue Service and to the Securities and Exchange Commission. These misrepresentations required the collusion of the marketplace and the accounting industry, so that investment houses and accounting firms such as Arthur Andersen also fell under the investigation of the Department of Justice.

Compounding the misery, many executives ran off with hundreds of millions of dollars of the illicit profits derived from selling disvalued shares, leaving employees and investors with huge losses. One source estimates that more than 94,000 jobs were lost and $2.67 billion was taken from corporate assets, much of it removed under questionable legality.[3]

No nation is any stronger than its economy. How to best manage the economy is one of society's oldest problems. Many societies choose to have government own the means of production. This method is called communism or "commonly owned." Many choose to assign ownership of the means of production to the private sector, except that the government would own the base means: coal, steel, and other sources of raw materials. This method is called socialism and has wide flexibility in application.

The United States chooses to leave the means of production entirely to the private sector. Hence, a collapse of the U.S. stock market is far more serious than the threat of impoverishment. The very fate of the nation can hang in the balance. Taking vigorous steps to restore investor confidence in the U.S. marketplace, Congress passed the Public Company Accounting Reform and Investor Protection Act of 2002. Popularly known as The Sarbanes-Oxley Act[4] or simply, "SOX," the law is named after its authors, Senator Paul Sarbanes (D-Maryland) and Representative Michael Oxley (R-Ohio).

As the term "public company" suggests in its title, SOX applies to corporations under the purview of the Securities and Exchange Commission (SEC). Composed of 11 titles as shown in figure 6.1, the act mandates strict requirements for the financial accounting of public companies, thereby transforming how the accounting industry does business, and reforms the disclosure procedures and governance of corporations. It also has limited application to private companies, to be discussed later in this book.

Each title of SOX contains several sections, which are numbered to correspond to their titles. For example, section 302 is located under title III; section 805 is located under title VIII. This format is standard for government acts and a particular law is usually referred to by both its section and title. Not all the sections of SOX are applicable to ISO 9001, although most of the titles can apply in some sense. In the remainder of this chapter, the financial meaning of the titles is described in brief by section, with some associated general comments so that the underlying message to management is made clear. Chapter 7 discusses governance within the context of SOX, and then follows up with a tie-in of SOX to ISO 9001.

Figure 6.1—The 11 titles of Sarbanes-Oxley

Title I—Public Company Accounting Oversight Board

Title II—Auditor Independence

Title III—Corporate Responsibility

Title IV—Enhanced Financial Disclosures

Title V—Analyst Conflicts of Interest

Title VI—Commission Resources and Authority

Title VII—Studies and Reports

Title VIII—Corporate and Criminal Fraud Accountability

Title IX—White-Collar Crime Penalty Enhancements

Title X—Corporate Tax Returns

Title XI—Corporate Fraud and Accountability

There are many sections to each title—a half dozen at least. Some of them are omitted in the descriptions that follow, either because they have no foreseeable relevance to ISO 9001, or because they're expansions and details of sections whose general descriptions are sufficient for the purposes of this book.

TITLE I: PUBLIC COMPANY ACCOUNTING OVERSIGHT BOARD

Section 101 establishes the Public Company Accounting Oversight Board, popularly called the PCAOB, to oversee the audit of public companies subject to the securities laws. The PCAOB is a nongovernmental agency operated as a nonprofit organization. It's tasked to:

- Register public accounting firms that prepare audit reports for public companies
- Establish rules for financial audits, ethics, and auditor independence
- Conduct inspections of registered public accounting firms, and conduct investigations and disciplinary proceedings
- Enforce compliance of the act

The remaining sections describe the procedures relevant to these responsibilities.

The focus of this title is on accounting firms and not on public companies per se. In other words, the usual procedure is for a public company to hire an accounting firm, which will then certify the company's books and aver to the value of the company. There are four levels in this hierarchy: the PCAOB, accounting firm, public company, and investor. Title I defines the relationship between the first two levels.

TITLE II: AUDITOR INDEPENDENCE

Section 201 prohibits an audit firm from simultaneously performing a non-audit service to an "issuer," a term that refers to a company that issues stock, that is, a public company. In this case, the issuer is a client of the audit firm and can be called a "client company." The client company can waive this restriction only if such waiver is announced to investors, and if the value of the non-audit service is less than 5 percent of the audit service. The latter rule is called a "de minimus exception" and is detailed in section 202. The exception recognizes that it's nearly impossible to perform a constructive audit without commenting on the structure of the thing audited, and that it's equally difficult to advise on structure without the perspective of an auditor. During either event, a certain amount of information is going to be exchanged and paid for. The purpose of the rule is to separate the essential activities of consulting and auditing as much as is reasonable.

Section 201 is derived from the collusion between Enron and Arthur Andersen, in which the latter advised Enron on its corporate structure and tax positions resulting from that structure, then came in as an auditor and declared that everything was fine. This arrangement meant that the audit firm was essentially auditing itself. Though such a practice has been common in the world of quality, it's widely regarded as unethical in the financial world; hence, the prohibition by SOX.

Section 203 rotates the lead auditor every five years. The purpose of this rule is fairly straightforward. Lead auditors have high visibility in a company being audited, and their favor is sought even if only to facilitate the audit. After a certain time, it's possible to groom the attitude of a lead auditor somewhat, in terms of disposition toward the company and in terms of the depth of exploration of the audit. SOX dictates that five years is that certain time.

Section 204 requires the team from the audit firm to report its rules and procedures to the issuer audit committee. SOX defines the audit committee as a committee established by the board of directors of the issuer for the purpose of overseeing its accounting and financial reporting processes and audits of its financial statements. If the board fails to establish such a committee, the entire board becomes the *de jure* audit committee. In any case, it seems both fair and reasonable that the audit team would inform the right people what they intend to audit and how they intend to do it. This process facilitates the audit and minimizes any adverse effect of the audit on company operations.

Section 206 deals with avoiding a conflict of interest between an audit firm and a client company. For example, imagine that an audit firm is hired to audit a client company. Suppose that an employee of the client company is a chief executive officer, controller, chief financial officer, chief accounting officer, or any person serving in an equivalent position. In other words, this executive person is in a position to make decisions that affect the value of the company. Finally, suppose that this executive person had been an employee of the audit firm at some time prior to being employed by the client company, and in that capacity had previously audited the client company. SOX prohibits this audit firm from conducting the audit.

This prohibition can be thought of as a "Caesar's wife" law. As Proconsul, Julius Caesar divorced his wife, whom he suspected of extra-marital activity, on the grounds that "Caesar's wife must be above suspicion." So also, an executive officer of a client company who recently worked for an audit firm must be above even the appearance of temptation.

Section 207 calls for the General Accounting Office (GAO) to conduct a study of the potential effects that would be caused by a mandatory rotation of audit firms that certify a given issuer. Needless to say, this recommendation is extremely controversial. William M. Sinnett reports that almost all of the large public accounting firms, the Fortune 1,000 companies and the companies' audit committee chairs believe that the costs of mandatory audit firm rotation were likely to exceed the benefits.[5] On the other hand, Sinnett says that at least one client company, and a big one at that—the California Public Employees Retirement System (CalPERS)—strongly supports the rotation of audit firms.

The pros and cons of such a rotation are clear and rather similar to the mandatory rotation of lead auditors. The argument in favor of audit firm rotation is this: Objectivity is reduced by familiarity. At Enron, Arthur Andersen auditors enjoyed their own private and permanent office, dressed as the Enron employees dressed, and even attended Enron parties.[6] This kind of closeness may be expected when, as the authors report, the average association of an audit firm and a client company is twenty-two years and can endure several generations, some of them having existed for more than seventy-five years. Eventually there's an erosion of independence as the audit team associates itself with the views and objectives of the client management. Added to this is the observation that familiarity leads to a lack of attention to detail due to staleness and redundancy.

The argument against the rotation of audit firms is this: The audit firm-client company relationship is a complex problem because it involves a major investment of time and money. Audit firms present statistics to show that first-year audit failure rates are high, and a mandatory rotation would therefore result in higher-than-usual adverse effects.[7] In addition, the very nature of auditing is one of mutual experience and cooperation between an auditor and auditee. Audit firms argue that professionalism is the answer, not rotation.

The battle rages on because so much money is at stake. The cost of mandatory rotation to the principles is great, but the cost to the public due to malfeasance is many times greater. The relationship between audit firms and public companies affects millions of investors.

The GAO concluded that "mandatory audit firm rotation may not be the most efficient way to enhance auditor independence and audit quality, considering the additional financial costs and the loss of institutional knowledge of a public company's previous auditor of record." The GAO then effectively postponed a difficult decision by recommending that both the SEC and the PCAOB continue to monitor the effectiveness of existing requirements for enhancing auditor independence and audit quality.[8]

Section 209 empowers state regulatory authorities to assess the appropriateness of the standard to accounting firms and businesses of various sizes. In particular, the standards applied by the PCAOB are not presumed applicable to small- and medium-sized nonregistered public accounting firms.

Intuitively, it makes sense that there be exceptions to the application of power, and SOX represents power. Consider the trivial case of a certified public accountant (CPA) who maintains the books for mom and pop grocery stores. Somewhere between this simple case and General Motors is a dividing line of SOX applicability. Section 209 assigns to the states the task of defining that dividing line. Most states license CPA activities and have the administrative structure and experience to carry out this task.

TITLE III: CORPORATE RESPONSIBILITY

Section 301 provides the responsibilities of the issuer audit committee. Each member of this committee will be a member of the board of directors, so that the audit committee is a direct committee of the executive board, and its accountability is unquestionable. The audit committee is responsible for the appointment, compensation, and oversight of any registered public accounting firm hired by the issuer for the purpose of preparing and issuing an audit report. This section ties the audit firm and the issuer closely in the work of an audit, effectively intertwining their responsibilities and accountability.

Section 302 is one of two certification requirements of SOX. (The other is section 906.) The certification required by this section will apply to every annual and quarterly report. The CEO and CFO must certify that:
- They've read the report, and to their knowledge it doesn't contain material misstatements or omissions.
- The financial information in the report fairly represents in all material respects the company's operations and financial condition.
- The certifying officers are responsible for establishing and maintaining internal controls.
- The effectiveness of the controls has been evaluated within the last ninety days.

The certification must report the officers' conclusions regarding the effectiveness of the controls, that they've reported to the auditors and the audit committee all significant deficiencies and material weaknesses in the controls, and whether there were significant changes in the internal controls subsequent to their evaluation date. This includes corrective actions taken with regard to significant deficiencies and material weaknesses.

This section reveals as much as any other about the effort that the writers of the law put into assigning accountability to corporate executive officers. An officer might sign an audit report revealed later to have been inaccurate. The alibi could be that he or she was unaware of the inaccuracies. But this alibi wouldn't be airtight because if an investigation revealed that ineffective control was the cause for the report error, the executive would then face a new charge of neglect.

Section 303 prohibits executive management from improper influence of an auditor in a financial audit report. Improper influence includes actions to influence, manipulate, coerce, or mislead any independent CPA hired by the issuer to perform an audit of financial statements, for the purpose of rendering the statements misleading.

Notice that the burden of proof of malfeasance would be on the plaintiff, as it should be. Audits have been known to rise to acrimonious levels, which can cause tempers to flare. An officer of the audited company could harass an auditor, or vice versa. Depending on the circumstances, either event could potentially stand by itself as a crime. But it would have no bearing on SOX unless the purpose of the harassment was to "render the statements misleading."

TITLE IV: ENHANCED FINANCIAL DISCLOSURES

Section 404 requires top management to establish and maintain an adequate system of internal financial controls, and to annually assess whether an internal control is effective. Moreover, an auditor from a registered accounting firm must attest to this assessment in the audit report.

The requirement placed on top management to verify the effectiveness of its internal control system has profound ramifications. It means that top management will literally have to go down to the counting room and verify controls. Suddenly, the ivory tower vanishes, and executive management becomes a hands-on job. The CEO can no longer use the excuse, "I didn't know. I left that to the people who work underneath me." Because the placement and structure of controls really does require a solid understanding of the system to be controlled, top management is accountable. This requirement presents a huge learning task, but isn't unreasonable. In Japan, top management has long had hands-on responsibility.

Section 406 requires a code of ethics for senior financial officers. Most professions have a code of ethics, as do many businesses. It could be argued that a code of ethics is an intrinsic part of professionalism. But even though ethics, morals, and laws have always guided human behavior, only the latter have generally been regarded as mandatory. This section is in the direction of moving at least some behaviors, formerly regarded as voluntary, into the purview of the law. A company gets to formulate its own code of ethics, which can be as rigorous or as inconsequential as they choose, but the major gain of the law is to invoke an ethical code of some sort. It can be toughened up in subsequent years if the performance falls short of the objective.

Section 409 requires real-time disclosure of material changes in the *financial condition or operations* of the issuer in financial reports. There's some ambiguity here, so the sentence has two interpretations:
a. Material changes in the financial condition or financial operations
b. Material changes in the financial condition or in issuer operations

At first glance, (a) seems to be the most likely reading, except that in the section, "condition" is singular and "operations" is plural, so that there is a contextual switch in sense. On the other hand, (b) suggests the scope of SOX will be broadened from strictly financial to general operations. This view is increasing in legal circles. For example, Christopher Myers and Lisa Kuca of the law firm Holland and Knight, use this wording: "The CEO and CFO of a public company under SOX purview must certify in their financial reports a fair presentation of the financial condition and results of operations of the company."[9] In either case, the report might influence market price and is properly within the purview of SOX.

TITLE V: ANALYST CONFLICTS OF INTEREST

Section 501 requires that securities associations and exchanges adopt rules to prevent analysts from making recommendations in their own interests and not in that of the investor. This section is derived from the scandals brought about by companies like Enron, which were compounded by processes in which brokers and advisors were recommending stock of companies known by insiders to be failing.

In many cases, the system of securities sales itself was the cause of this malfeasance. Riches could be obtained by unethical but legal selling. If a broker knew, for example, the closing price of a stock in one part of the world, while working in a region where the market was still open, money could be made even though it might mean a loss for the investor. It's not always a simple matter to adopt rules tying the broker's profits to those of the investor, but such rules are absolutely necessary, given human weakness.

TITLE VI: COMMISSION RESOURCES AND AUTHORITY

This title refers to the SEC, authorizing that body additional funds with which to exercise its responsibilities vis-à-vis SOX. The title also provides the authority to set professional standards and qualifications for those who appear before the commission, and for those who exercise the positions of brokers, advisors, and dealers in securities.

This title "tidies up" the authority of the SEC in areas that may have been ethical issues prior to SOX but are now matters of regulation. By its very nature, the stock market is a place of opportunity and pragmatism. The SEC's job is to ensure fairness and proper behavior in the marketplace. Those who could anticipate the ingenuity of humans in self-gain will always lag behind stray practice. From time to time, new laws are required to tidy up the arena, and SOX is one of those laws.

TITLE VII: STUDIES AND REPORTS

This title refers to tasking the Comptroller General to study the consolidation and operation of public accounting firms. During the years, such firms have decreased in number, resulting in less competition among them, higher costs, lower quality of services, and diminishment of auditor independence. Title VII also calls for a similar study of the operation of investment banks, the nature of violations, and the means of enforcement. Recommendations resulting from the studies are requested that will help to resolve the problems. For example, the Comptroller General is specifically requested to look for ways to increase competition among the firms.

TITLE VIII: CORPORATE AND CRIMINAL FRAUD ACCOUNTABILITY

Title VIII differs from the others in that it applies to both public and private companies.[10] It refers to the destruction of valid records and the creation of fraudulent ones; the retention of records; whistle-blowing protection and threats and harassment of employees; and criminal penalties.

Section 802 provides criminal penalties for altering documents, records, or tangible objects with the intent to impede, obstruct, or influence an investigation by an authorized agency of the United States. In this sense, altering includes destroying, mutilating, concealing, covering-up, or falsifying any document, record, or tangible object.

Section 806 can be called the "whistle-blowers protection law." It protects employees of publicly traded companies who provide evidence of fraud by prohibiting any officer, employee, agent, or subcontractor of a company from taking adverse action against an employee who has provided information to or has assisted in an investigation into what the employee believes is a violation of law. In this sense, adverse action constitutes dismissal, demotion, suspension, threat, harassment, or other discrimination. The importance of section VIII can't be emphasized enough.

Fear has been a management tactic for centuries and remains so today. W. Edwards Deming condemned the practice as recently as 1986, espousing freedom from fear as one of his 14 points for management.[11] Strictly speaking, the law refers to whistle-blowers of financial matters, but it can easily be extended to fraud in any part of the company because it encompasses "fraud against shareholders." As an example, doctoring a product to conceal a defect, then selling the defective product to a customer is fraud within the purview of SOX, whether or not this fraud is covered up in financial accounts or is simply unreported.

TITLE IX: WHITE-COLLAR CRIME PENALTY ENHANCEMENTS

Sections 902 through 905 prohibit attempts and conspiracies to commit fraud, and they define associated penalties. However, the section that has the greatest potential application to quality is section 906, which is the other of two certification requirements of SOX (the first is section 302). Section 906 is a criminal provision with heavy fines and imprisonment.

It requires that each periodic report containing financial statements filed pursuant to the Securities and Exchange Act of 1934 will be accompanied by a certification of the CEO and CFO that the report fully complies and fairly represents in all material respects, the financial condition and results of operations of the company. Section 906 differs from section 302 in that its certification is absolute, with no "knowledge" or "materiality" qualifier. However, criminal penalties are reserved for those who certify their financial report while knowing that the report doesn't comply with the requirements.

It's clear that companies will now have to pay even closer attention to their financial statement, due diligence procedures, and internal controls—which is exactly the intent of SOX. The principle of interest here is the tie-in of accountability of top management to the truth of a report written at a lower level in the corporate hierarchy. As with titles III and IV, SOX is aimed at outmaneuvering the plea of innocence from top management.

TITLE X: CORPORATE TAX RETURNS

This title requires the CEO to sign the corporate income tax statement. Title X isn't an issue of concern to this book because it has no apparent connection, nor any analogy, to the requirements of ISO 9001.

TITLE XI: CORPORATE FRAUD AND ACCOUNTABILITY

Section 1102 is an extension of title VIII where records or documents are destroyed or altered to impair an official proceeding. This section appears to attack malfeasance coming and going. If a person fraudulently alters a record, he or she has broken the law. If the investigation needed the record in the pursuit of its business, the law has been broken again. The symmetry of squeeze is exquisite. Suppose that someone falsifies a record, and then destroys it upon finding out that investigators are coming. No fraudulent record exists, but if someone else observed that person destroying the record, he or she would still be guilty of breaking the law.

Section 1107 prohibits retaliation against informants and is an extension of section 806, which protects whistle-blowers. It seems to be a more general application. Every whistle-blower is an informant as well as employee. An informant might not be an employee of the offending company, but someone from outside with information vital to the investigation. That informant is equally protected before the law.

REFERENCES

1. "A Bird's-Eye View of the Enron Debacle." *American Institute of Certified Public Accountants,* www.aicpa.org, Jan. 13, 2005.
2. Nocera, Joseph. "System Failure: Corporate America Has Lost Its Way." *Fortune,* June 24, 2001.
3. "U.S. Corporate Excess: The Barons of Bankruptcy." *Financial Facts Multi-*

media, Limited, www.finfacts.com, Aug. 1, 2002.
4. H.R. 3763, *The Sarbanes-Oxley Act of 2002.* 107th Congress of the United States of America, Washington, D.C., Jan. 23, 2002.
5. Sinnett, William M. "Are There Good Reasons for Auditor Rotation?" *The Financial Executive,* Oct. 2004.
6. Arel, Barbara, Richard G. Brody, and Kurt Pany. "Audit Firm Rotation and Audit Quality." *The CPA Journal,* Jan. 2005.
7. Ibid.
8. Op. cit. Sinnet, William M.
9. Myers, Christopher and Lisa Kuca. "Government Regulation: SEC, Fraud, Whistle-Blowing, and How You Can Protect Your Company." Presentation of Holland & Knight LLP. *Beyond Compliance to Sarbanes-Oxley: Financial Benefits from Integrating Your Managemnt Systems.* American Society for Quality symposium, Philadelphia, September 27–28, 2005.
10. Lieberman, Larry D. "Sarbanes-Oxley Affects Your Private Company Clients." *Wisconsin Lawyer,* Vol. 77, No. 6, June 2004.
11. Deming, W. Edwards. *Out of the Crisis.* Massachusetts Institute of Technology, Center for Advanced Engineering Study, 1986.

CHAPTER 7

SARBANES-OXLEY AND GOVERNANCE

Sarbanes-Oxley (SOX) isn't a standard; it's an act of legislation. It tells you what to do but provides no guidelines on how to do it. A study of the document shows it to be all about governance, as defined in chapter 4, yet nowhere is the word "governance" found in SOX. The act is very explicit on its requirement for financial internal controls, though it doesn't define them, either. The challenge, then, is to find common ground between a generally accepted view of corporate governance and the SOX requirements for financial internal controls. In keeping with the spirit of the law, any definitions that are adopted for this purpose should reflect the ethical objectives of SOX. The days of corporate laissez faire are over. In keeping with the spirit of this book, the common ground must be in regard to principles—corporate governance and internal controls—not just financial controls.

INTERNAL CONTROLS

Fortunately, much work in this direction has already been done. For example, the Securities and Exchange Commission (SEC) accepts the definition of internal controls provided by the Committee of Sponsoring Organizations of the Treadway Commission (COSO) because it's applicable to all corporate functions and operations.[1] COSO gives the following definition of internal control: "a process designed to provide reasonable assurance regarding the achievement of objectives in the following categories: effectiveness and efficiency of operations, reliability of financial reporting; compliance with applicable laws and regulations."[2]

COSO adds important qualifications to this definition, recognizing that internal controls have their limitations. They can help achieve performance targets and ensure reliable reporting. They can help ensure compliance with laws and regulations. But they can't change a poor manager into a good one. They can't ensure success, nor necessarily accommodate shifts in policy, programs, competition, or economic conditions. In short, internal controls can only provide reasonable assurance to management regarding achievement of objectives. These shortcomings occur in all human-machine systems because of faulty judgment, bad decisions, mistakes, resource constraints, and mischief.

Nevertheless, COSO asserts that an internal control system goes a long way to proper governance when supplemented with five components:
- Control environment
- Control activity
- Risk management
- Information and communication
- Monitoring and measuring[3]

These components are strikingly similar to the requirements of governance of ISO 9001 presented in chapter 5. Thus, we've found common ground between the governance requirements of SOX and ISO 9001 and will describe these components in the following divisions.

CONTROL ENVIRONMENT

The control environment is defined by the factors that provide direction and establish degrees of freedom in which to operate. This is the component traditionally seen as top management responsibility. COSO declares it to be the "foundation of internal control," providing discipline and structure. Many of the factors of the control environment are identical to those of ISO 9001, including requirements for competence of employees; assignment of authority and responsibility; resource allocation; company organization; and corporate goals, policies, and leadership. The control environment also includes some of the guidelines from ISO 9004, such as concerns for integrity, ethical values, and management philosophy and operating style.

Figure 7.1 associates the factors of the COSO control environment to related clauses of ISO 9001 or ISO 9004. If a control environment factor matches up with both ISO standards, which is the general case, then only the association to ISO 9001 is given because it's the only factor that can be contractually required.

CONTROL ACTIVITY

The control activity is defined by the factors that get things done. Whereas the control environment is largely the purview of top management, the control activity spans the company vertically and horizontally. This means that all levels of the company hierarchy and all of its functions are engaged in control activities. As with the control environment, many of the factors of the control activity can be found in diverse ISO 9001 requirements—such as for planning, procedures, process organization, correction, prevention, development, training, and assessment. Authorizations, validation, verification, and reviews also come under control activity.

Figure 7.1—Control environment factors matched with ISO 9001 requirements

Control environment factor	ISO 9001 requirement
Competence	6.2.2
Responsibility and authority	5.5.1
Resource utilization	6.1
Organization	4.1; 5.1
Goals, policy, leadership	5.1; 5.3; 5.4 4.3 (9004)
Integrity, ethical values	5.2; 5.3 (9004)
Management philosophy, operating style	5.0 (all)

Figure 7.2—Control activity factors matched with ISO 9001 requirements

Control activity factor	ISO 9001 requirement
Planning	7.1; 7.2
Procedures	7.3; 7.5
Process organization	7.0 (all subclauses)
Correction and prevention	8.5
Training and development	6.2
Assessment, validation, verification	8.2; 8.4; 7.1; 7.5.2
Authorizations	4.2; 5.6.3; 7.4; 8.3
Reviews	5.6

Source: Committee of Sponsoring Organizations of the Treadway Commission. Enterprise Risk Management Framework, 1994. Reprinted with permission of AICPA.

Figure 7.2 associates the factors of the COSO control activity to related clauses of ISO 9001 or ISO 9004. As with the previous figure, if a control activity factor matches up with both ISO standards, only the association to ISO 9001 is given. The associations are based upon the relatively general statements of governance issued by COSO. However, this preliminary match-up suggests that a more detailed description would yield a more detailed association. The objective of this table and others like it is to show that the two standards, ISO 9001 and COSO's Internal Control Integrated Framework, are in mutual compliance.

Information and Communication

The modus operandi throughout this book is to show parallels of interest between ISO 9000 and SOX. This entails drawing upon principles because SOX is specifically aimed at financial controls and cites principles and standards in those terms. The subject of information and communication is a case in point. SOX is concerned with records, reports, audits, and documentation aimed at financial control. Many of the authorities of pertinent standards acknowledge that this view is too narrow to be implemented in an effective way, and they address control principles that could be applicable to general corporate operations.

Many can agree that in the global economy, managing information has risen to a prominent position in any company that hopes to be successful. In recent years, this interest has been expressed in various terms; database management, management information systems, information management, and knowledge management are just a few. Many companies have responded to the importance of the matter by creating chief information officers (CIO) with vice-presidential visibility.

Market research, production scheduling, payroll, bill of materials file, the general ledger, personnel records, and accounts receivable are just a few of the types of information used on a daily basis in most companies. The purpose of managing information is to keep it current and readily available to users. Computers help enormously in this task, but a CIO is also needed. Users will want to control the information, but the CIO must control the system. For example, the CIO is responsible for connectivity, a characteristic of the system that refers to how well computers and computer-based devices can communicate with one another.

ISO 9001 is concerned with information management as a process, so its requirements are directed to the following necessary and sufficient issues:
- Identification of information needs and sources
- Timely access to adequate information
- Use of information for strategies and objectives
- Appropriate security and confidentiality

All of these issues are equally important to COSO's internal control standard, which uses very similar terms:

"Pertinent information must be identified, secured, and communicated in a form and timeframe that enable people to carry out their responsibilities. Information systems produce reports, containing operational, financial and compliance-related information, that make it possible to run and control the business. They deal not only with internally generated data, but also information about external events, activities, and conditions necessary to informed business decision-making and external reporting. Effective communication also must occur in a broader sense, flowing down, across, and up the organization. All personnel must receive a clear message from top management that control responsibilities must be taken seriously. They must understand their own role in the internal control system, as well as how individual activities relate to the work of others. They must have a means of communicating significant information upstream. There also needs to be effective communication with external parties, such as customers, suppliers, regulators and shareholders."[4]

Although SOX is primarily concerned with financial documentation, the law recognizes that in modern corporations, this information is embedded in its information technology (IT). Therefore, many interpreters of the law conclude that a company's IT system falls under the purview of SOX. If a company's IT system is extensive, it might want to consider a formal standard devoted directly to that end. The IT Governance Institute (ITGI) and the Information Systems Audit and Control Association (ISACA) provide such a standard. It's called "Control Objectives for Information Technology" and is often abbreviated as CobIT. Figure 7.3 associates the COSO information factors to ISO 9001 requirements. One of the factors is a guideline of ISO 9004.

CobIT

Control shouldn't be dismissed for having too narrow a focus on business operations because the tide is going the other way. SOX is driving all publicly held enterprises to reorganize around internal controls. Pragmatic and results-oriented methods such as the Malcolm Baldrige National Quality Award criteria, Six Sigma, and lean, will eventually accommodate this reality. CobIT does, and ISO 9001 always did.

CobIT has identified 34 controls necessary for an effective and secure IT system. They're structured around four basic types of operations:
- Planning and organization
- Acquisition and implementation
- Monitoring and evaluation
- Delivery and support

These aren't controls in a restrictive sense; on the contrary, they're effective checklists of the processes that are required for effective and efficient IT. They

Figure 7.3—Information and communication factors matched with ISO 9001

Information and communication factor	ISO 9001 requirement
Identification of needs and sources	4.2; 5.1; 5.4; 6.3; 7.3; 7.5
Timely access and adequacy	4.2.3; 5.5; 7.2; 7.4.2
Use for strategy and objectives	4.1; 5.3; 8.4
Security and confidentiality	6.5 (9004)

tell you what must be done to say that you're doing the right thing. In other words, they're a validation of your IT system.

Risk Management

Risk is the uncertainty in achieving a goal. It's a probability—a number between zero and one. Risk management is a discipline for dealing with uncertainty and refers to identification, assessment, and control of impediments or barriers to the goals. As an example, suppose that you want to maintain a given debt-equity ratio or achieve a given inventory turnover. What are the risks in doing so, and what controls can you put in place to ensure acceptable risk?

The Risk Management Center identifies four steps in dealing with risks:
1. Establish the context.
2. Identify the risks.
3. Evaluate and prioritize them.
4. Implement a risk management program.[5]

Establishing the context simply means examining the goal and identifying potential barriers and/or impediments.

Identifying risks is made easier by developing a strategy for the various categories of risks: people, property, income, and goodwill. Evaluating and prioritizing the risks is essential to keeping costs in control. You associate a probability with each risk, which sets up a kind of Pareto selection process to deal with the greater risks first. Then you develop a risk management program that defines strategies and processes for minimizing the occurrence or effect of risks.

Figure 7.4 connects the factors of risk management to the guidelines of ISO 9004. As with the previous charts in this chapter, the ISO 9004 requirements refer to the clause in the document shown in the heading, unless otherwise indicated.

Figure 7.4—Risk management factors matched with ISO 9004

Risk management factor	ISO 9004 guidelines
Establish the context	4.1; 5.1 (9001)
Identify the risks	5.1.2; 5.6.2; 6.3; 7.3.1; 7.4.1
Evaluate and prioritize	5.4.2; 8.2.2 (9004); 8.5 (9001)
Implement risk management program	5.4.2; 6.3; 7.4.1; 7.5.2 (9004) 8.5 (9001)

MONITORING AND MEASURING

This component of COSO refers to the policies, procedures, and processes that are set up to achieve goals and deal with risks. Quality systems are generally designed to deal with risks, although we don't often think of them in this context. For example, a Shewhart control chart is a risk indicator. It provides a measurement relative to a target value and a probability associated with the measurement. A correction system is effectively a risk management program, which is why clause 8.5 of ISO 9001 is listed in figure 7.4. It's effectively, if not explicitly, risk management.

At this time, SOX holds top management legally responsible for the effectiveness and efficiency of its financial processes. It should be noted that the requirements of SOX could, in principle, extend beyond finance to any operation in the company. As with the other components of COSO governance, focus is placed on the factors of monitoring and measurement as they might be applied to other company activities. This clarifies the similarity of the COSO component to the monitoring and measuring requirements of ISO 9001.

COSO's use of the word "monitoring" means that internal control systems are observed and evaluated to assess the quality of the system's performance over time. Monitoring is ongoing during the course of operations, with deficiencies and other serious matters reported to top management. COSO uses "measuring" to mean that operations are evaluated in real time for effectiveness and efficiency. Effectiveness is a measure of the extent to which planned activities are realized and planned results achieved. Efficiency is a measure of the relation between results achieved and resources used.[6] The degree to which planned activities, results, and resources all meet or exceed customer expectations indicates how well the system is performing. Therefore, effectiveness and

Figure 7.5—Monitoring and measuring factors associated with ISO 9001 requirements

Monitoring and measuring factor	ISO 9001 requirement
Establish criteria; define metrics	4.1; 8.2
Measure control system performance	8.2
Assess effectiveness and efficiency	8.3; 8.4
Improve control system	8.5

efficiency are necessary and sufficient measures of quality system improvement. Figure 7.5 relates the factors of the COSO monitoring and measurement component to those of ISO 9001.

REFERENCES

1. *Management's Reports on Internal Control Over Financial Reporting and Certification of Disclosure in Exchange Act Periodic Reports,* Securities and Exchange Commission, RIN 3235-AI66 and 3235-AI79, Aug. 14, 2003.
2. Committee of Sponsoring Organizations of the Treadway Commission. *Enterprise Risk Management Framework.* Jersey City, N.J.: American Institute of Certified Public Accountants, 2004.
3. Committee of Sponsoring Organizations of the Treadway Commission. *Internal Control—Integrated Framework Executive Summary.* 1985–2004.
4. Ibid.
5. "Introduction to the Risk Management Process." *Nonprofit Risk Management Center, www.nonprofitrisk.org,* Aug. 15, 2001.
6. ANSI/ISO/ASQ. Q9000-2000. *Quality Management Systems—Fundamentals and Vocabulary.* Milwaukee: ASQ, 2000.

CHAPTER 8

AN ISO 9001 FORMAT FOR SARBANES-OXLEY

The massive and widespread scandals of 2000, in which financial accounting in the United States was shown to be out of control, led to the Sarbanes-Oxley Act of 2002 (SOX). In the last chapter, it was clear that SOX was written expressly to restore corporate accounting practices to good order. The law focuses on public companies because it was the resultant major collapse of the stock market that threatened the U.S. economy. A society is only as stable as its economy, and business practices can't be completely laissez faire. Corporate governance of financial matters must be in control and operated according to ethical and regulatory standards.

It would be unfortunate, though, if a company were to accept this mandate too narrowly. Charles Cobb points out that such a narrow view occurred with the advent of the ISO 9000 standard series during the late 1980s.[1] Everyone rushed to meet the minimum requirements of the auditors and missed a great opportunity to add business value. ISO 9000's reputation is still recovering from this underutilization. Cobb recommends a new structure with an integrated management system that goes beyond compliance with SOX to accommodate other quality and regulatory requirements.

Authors Sandford Liebesman and Paul Palmes also recommend an integrated approach to satisfy the financial, environmental, and quality requirements of SOX, ISO 14001, and ISO 9001, respectively.[2] Critics may claim that financial and environmental requirements are the law and quality is not. This is true, but misses the point. If all you want to do is not break the law, simply shut down operations and go home. Presumably, you're in business to make money, and you do that by providing a product or service to customers. This is precisely what quality is all about.

SYSTEMS INTEGRATION

Quality isn't cosmetic. A company provides a service or product, and to survive must do this effectively, efficiently, and systematically. If it does all of these things well, as perceived by the customer, that's quality. Any other interpretation of quality is a misunderstanding. ISO 9001 provides a framework to enhance the systematic approach to effectiveness and efficiency.

SOX has requirements for internal control of financial accounting systems but doesn't provide an operational framework. ISO 9001, however, has similar requirements for quality and *does* provide an operational framework. It's reasonable for those companies that are ISO 9001-certified to adapt SOX requirements to this framework. As one example, ISO 9001 offers a single and complete set of managed and applied procedures, which are distributed where needed, regularly updated, and audited. SOX has identical requirements for policies and procedures for financial accounting systems. Therefore, SOX requirements are eminently adaptable to the ISO 9001 documentation framework.

Jim Mroz, senior editor of *The Informed Outlook*, agrees with this idea, saying it would be relatively simple to piggyback accounting procedures, processes, and audits on an existing ISO 9001 framework.[3] Mroz points out that by emulating and integrating ISO 9001 in all their financial and information activities, companies can gain compliance with SOX and achieve a seamless and effective integration of all critical corporate activity.

ISO 9001 and COSO share similar requirements in auditing, review, adherence to statutes and regulations, and involvement of executive management. It's both possible and reasonable to fit accounting and quality into one system of governance with similar policies, procedures, audits, measurements, and controls. This integration provides clarity, understanding, and transparency.

Figure 8.1 shows how a financial accounting system might be integrated with an ISO 9001 system of governance. In some cases, the map is straightforward—

Figure 8.1—Financial accounting system implemented in an ISO 9000 framework

Financial accounting subsystem	ISO 9001 quality management system
Accounting rules	4.2 Documentation (5.2.3: 9004)
Accounts payable/receivable	4.2 Documentation
Cash flow	5.0 Management responsibility (6.8: 9004)
Consolidated accounts	4.2 Documentation
Expense management	6.0 Resource management (6.8: 9004)
Fixed assets	6.3 Infrastructure
General ledger	4.2 Documentation
Inventory	6.0 Resource management
Marketable securities	5.0 Management responsibility (6.8: 9004)
Market value (company)	5.1 Management responsibility (5.2.3: 9004)
Payroll	5.0 Management responsibility (6.8: 9004)
Purchasing	7.4 Purchasing

purchasing is a good example. In other cases, ISO 9004 guidelines are useful. For example, clause 6.8 of ISO 9004 doesn't exist in ISO 9001. This doesn't mean you can't use it explicitly; on the contrary, ISO 9004 is at your service. But once it's put into a quality manual, it becomes an intrinsic part of the ISO 9001-based quality management system (QMS) and is contractual. Your customers don't contract with ISO, but with you, and your quality manual is your commitment.

SOX firmly and explicitly requires a public company to report its true market value. There's no equivalent requirement in either ISO 9001 or ISO 9004, and it might appear that ISO is unresponsive to this critical issue. However, ISO 9001, clause 5.1, Management commitment, and ISO 9004, clause 5.2.3, Statutory and regulatory requirements, do require management adherence to statutes and regulations. They provide the framework for the accounting system to confirm *its* responsibility to the requirements.

Neither the financial system nor the financial managers lose anything in this arrangement. They still manage the finance system—policies, procedures, and controls. Finance is no more subservient to quality than is the production, purchasing, comptroller, operations, or any other function within the company. What they gain is what everybody else gains: a format, reference, and comprehensive guide to requirements. The company is the big winner, gaining a single system of governance. Everyone is under one tent. One document describes the totality of the company's management effort: formerly the quality manual, now the governance manual. If the company is subject to, or volunteers for, environmental rules and considerations, it too would fit neatly into the governance system.

Figure 8.2 expands this broad view in more detail in terms of action items. If a company were subject to both SOX and ISO 9001, these actions would be taken by personnel looking after each standard independently, perhaps even simultaneously without them knowing. Why should two teams work incoherently to similar ends? Why not create a single management system? Audits can then be arranged according to a conformable schedule. Procedures could be uniform so that auditors can quickly assess references, procedures, and work instructions. Even plans could have a standard format, again for quick comparison, and as a check on comprehensiveness.

As a simple example, every plan should describe its references, resources, and schedule, or in general terms, the what, why, how, where, who, and when of things. When a plan is written in a standard format, decision makers, sponsors, auditors, and project leaders can quickly verify that the plan is complete. A central manager, such as a CEO who must read plans from diverse functions, benefits particularly from uniformity. The task is twofold: read the plan and then evaluate it. Both tasks are made easier when the plan uses a standard format.

It should come as no surprise that the COSO action items shown in figure 8.2 are identical to action items required by ISO 9001. You begin with a plan and then implement it. There's a standard way to go about this that doesn't derive from wizened heads but from pragmatists in the field. I'm reminded of the consultant who recounted how his company had been tasked to determine an algorithm for switching box cars in a railroad yard. Though they used the latest theories from operations research, they could find no better way to do it than the way it was being done—a tried-and-true method that had evolved from sweat and tears.

In the world of evolution, things either work or they fail. Ideas and problem solving are both similar in that aspect. You can go to the literature and find a half-

An ISO 9001 Format for Sarbanes-Oxley 75

Figure 8.2—COSO action items mapped into an ISO 9000 format

COSO action item	ISO 9001 requirement
Write accounting plan	7.1
Identify financial processes	7.5
Determine objectives and risks	4.1; 5.1
Establish control system	7.5
Write procedures	4.2.1
Establish audit program	8.2.2
Write audit plan	8.2.2
Establish training program	6.2.2
Implement improvement system	8.5

dozen problem-solving algorithms, but they all boil down to a similar process. J. E. Gibson[4] describes a general approach to problem solving that's virtually identical to the method described by C. J. Guffey and M. M. Helms[5] of the Tennessee Valley Authority, S. Feinberg[6] of Plessy Semiconductors, K. Bemowski[7] of Ford Motor Co., and D. V. Shaw et al.[8] of the Strong Memorial Hospital of Rochester, New York. The basic iteration is to identify a problem, analyze the problem, evaluate alternate solutions, select and implement a solution, and evaluate results. Moreover, a little wordsmithing will show that this algorithm is virtually identical to that of the famous DMAIC process of Six Sigma: define, measure, analyze, improve, and control.[9]

The actions of figure 8.2 also fit this algorithm and seem to be a pragmatic confirmation of the agreement of COSO and ISO 9001. They also reveal an obvious conclusion—a company can merge its financial management system and QMS into a single system of governance with similar policies, procedures, measurements, audits, and controls. The immediate benefit is to enable auditors to quickly and easily identify the company's compliance to SOX requirements by implementing the COSO rules on the world-renowned format of ISO 9001.

STATUTES AND REGULATIONS

I've previously referred to clause 5.1, Management commitment, referring to its statement on management's need to "communicate to the organization" the importance of meeting statutory and regulatory requirements. It's worthwhile to expand on this notion because, depending upon the products or services offered, a company could easily gloss over this statement and render its ISO 9001 framework unworkable for SOX. The company financial system *must* follow statutory and regulatory requirements. The company quality system might not need to do so.

According to ISO 9001, every company must have a methodology in place to identify, maintain, and update all applicable statutory and regulatory requirements. This requirement is explicit in clause 7.2, Customer-related processes; clause 7.3, Design and development; and, more important, clause 5.1, Management commitment. Why is clause 5.1 more important? In some cases, the company's products and services may not be subject to statutes and regulations, making clause 7.2 nonapplicable. In other cases, the company may have no design function, and therefore its quality system will have an exemption from clause 7.3.

Yet, the company infrastructure and work environment may well be subject to Occupational Safety and Health Administration (OSHA) regulations concerning, for example, lighting, heating and cooling, and safety issues. Perhaps the company must choose its suppliers from an approved list. This is particularly true where it uses toxic chemicals whose manufacturers are subject to statutory control. Invariably, a company may be subject to some sort of rule or regulation. In any case, clause 5.1 always applies.

Even the absence of statutory and regulatory requirements must be verified, so that the need for the company to have a methodology for this determination is always there. Hence, if a company has an ISO 9001-based QMS, the framework is in place for use by the company financial and accounting system to assign all of its criteria.

Consider the advantage an ISO 9001 framework gives you when the SOX auditors arrive. They'll be interested in your compliance to these requirements and your response can be: "Yes, we're in compliance to SOX, and our program is documented with policies and procedures in the appropriate clauses of our governance manual." Auditors appreciate and respect this kind of readiness.

REFERENCES

1. Cobb, Charles. "Sarbanes-Oxley: Pain or Gain?" *Quality Progress*, Nov. 2004, pp. 48–52.
2. Liebesman, Sandford, and Paul Palmes. "Quality's Path to the Boardroom."

Quality Progress, Oct. 2003, pp. 41–43.
3. Stanek, Steve. "Can ISO Standards Help in Today's Business Climate?" *Knowledge Leader*, Protiviti Corp., April 2, 2004. Quote of Jim Mroz, editor of *The Informed Outlook,* International Forum for Management Systems Inc.
4. Gibson, J. E. *How to Do Systems Analysis.* Charlottesville, Virginia, School of Engineering, University of Virginia workbook, 1990.
5. Guffey, C. J., and M. M. Helms. "The IRS and TVA are Leading the Way." *Quality Progress*, Oct. 1995, pp. 51–55.
6. Feinberg, S. "Overcoming the Real Issues of TQM Implementation." *Quality Progress*, July 1995, pp. 79–81.
7. Bemowski, K. "Ford Chairman Was, and Continues to Be, a Progress Chaser." *Quality Progress*, Oct. 1994, pp. 29–32.
8. Shaw, D. V., D. O. Day, and E. Slavinskas. "Learning from Mistakes." *Quality Progress*, June 1995, pp. 45–48.
9. *Six Sigma Quality.* GE Fanuc brochure, GE Co., 1998.

CHAPTER 9

FINANCIAL MEASURES OF QUALITY

Successful businesses take the strategic view of things—the big picture. They consider their roles in the marketplace, in business, and in society. James Collins and Jerry Porras of Stanford University call them visionary companies.[1] Driven by core values and a sense of purpose, they're able to adapt to the global picture. Their core values are who they are and what they can do. The implication here is that the strategic view is both interior and exterior—you must know who you are and what business you're in. Practically speaking, visionary leaders see all of their operations as a cohesive part of their identity. Production, human resources, and sales are all part of that identity. But the identity also includes the quality of their performance.

The converse of the visionary company is the corporation that takes the narrow view of its role in society. Eliyahu Goldratt and Jeff Cox were quoted in chapter 4 as saying that the goal of a company is singular—to make money. This is a powerful argument because over the short term it leads to shareholder satisfaction and CEO enrichment. But focusing on profits can be myopic because the interest of top management is on returns in the current quarter, whereas customer retention, global positioning, product development, and the emerging market all occur over the long term. Hence, the narrow view of business naturally leads to shortsighted conclusions and bad decisions.

The importance of vision is easily demonstrated by comparing two similar companies that started at about the same time. During the early 1900s, they were doing a comparable volume of business: The Estey Organ Co. of Vermont and the Klann Organ Co. of Virginia. Each company used the same approach in manufacturing—a craft-oriented business employing a relatively few, highly specialized workers. Estey went out of business in the 1950s. The Klann company, seeing further into the future, continues to make handcrafted organs in one part of its plant. The major part of the plant is devoted to injection molding, as the company is now the Klann Plastics Corp. of Waynesboro, Virginia.

The lack of strategic vision is manifested every day on issues that may appear simple but in fact can have grave consequences if perceived incorrectly. As an example, companies that lack vision commonly hold two misconceptions about current issues. The first misconception is that quality refers only to quality assurance; the second is that the Sarbanes-Oxley (SOX) Act refers only to financial processes. The idea that quality is about quality assurance is regrettably common and results in a typical scenario: the quality manager with the dubious distinction of a direct, dotted-line connection to the CEO, but with no authority. In companies that focus on today's profits, it's often cynically said of their front office staff that, among equals, the production manager is more equal than the others. One might add that the quality manager is less equal than the others.

We want to avoid making the same mistake about SOX. The new law presents more than the opportunity to take the strategic view. The prudent manager will see in this new law that the strategic approach is necessary because inevitably the SOX perspective will broaden to include operations. This will happen because of the cost of quality.

Although it's true that the "cost of quality" refers to quality processes, the latter don't apply to quality assurance, if they ever did. With the advent of ISO 9001:2000, "quality processes" refers to all the value-adding processes of production and service within the company, and can be construed to apply to its support services as well. Thus, the cost of quality permeates a company and has a direct influence on its bottom line, which under section 302 of SOX must be honestly reported upon pain of criminal penalty. At some given level of aggregation, the various activities of a company sum to unity, and that level is corporate governance. One can't plead, "I'm responsible for this operation but not that one." Top management is responsible for all of them.

Figure 9.1—The cost-versus-quality curve

[Graph: Cost of Quality (vertical axis) versus Degree of Conformance (horizontal axis, Low to High). Efficiency arrow points down, Effectiveness arrow points right. Curves shown for Total cost, Preventive cost, and Corrective cost.]

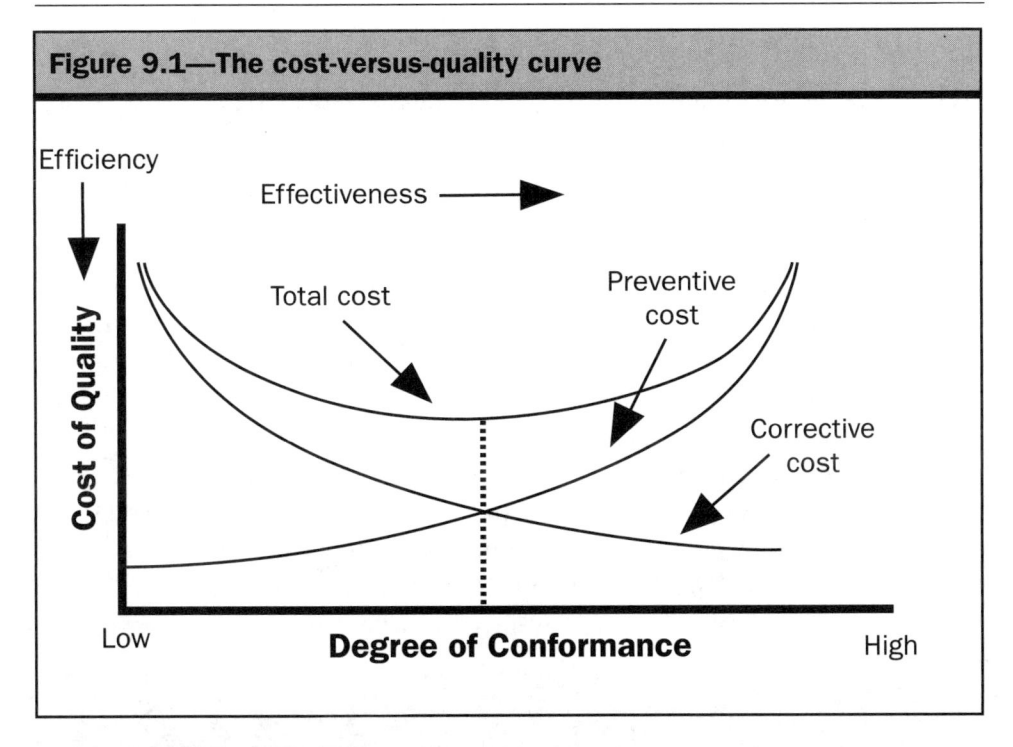

COST OF QUALITY

According to British Standard 4778, the cost of quality is the expenditure incurred by the producer, user, and community associated with product or service quality. This is as good a definition of the cost of quality as you'll find anywhere. It reflects the Japanese view of quality as a concern of society, and it satisfies our technical and philosophical notions of what quality is all about.

Figure 9.1 explains the cost of quality in terms of preventive and corrective costs. The "degree of conformance" on the horizontal axis refers to how well a product or service conforms to its target value; the higher the conformity, the higher the quality. As the quality of the output improves, the cost of correction decreases because there's less to correct, but preventive costs go up. Steps have to be taken to prevent defective work, and those steps cost money. For example, increased vigilance, better tests and test equipment, increased training of operators, and improved processes all contribute to improved quality. But despite being corporate investments, they add to cash outlay.

Conversely, saving on preventive costs lowers the degree of conformance and results in an increase of corrective costs. Sampling rates increase, as do repair, regrade, and scrap costs. The total cost curve is the algebraic sum of the preventive and corrective curves and always has an optimal value—the crossover point of the prevention and correction curves. You can push down the total cost curve through efficiencies, but sooner or later you reach diminishing returns. There's always optimal operation, inescapably requiring a judgment on the part of management about consumer and producer risks.

Joseph M. Juran recognized that the technical language of production, such as defect rates, out-of-specs, and failure modes, would probably not attract the attention of top management. He advocated a cost-of-quality accounting system in which costs could be put into categories that would be expressed in financial terms.[2] The categories are: failure, appraisal, and prevention, sometimes referred to as FAP. Figure 9.2 lists some of the common factors of costs, and a cursory look shows that a cost can easily be measured for each factor.

Many of the factors in figure 9.2 are quickly understood; a few need some explanation. In the category of failure, "regrade" refers to the loss incurred by reclassifying a defective top-of-the-line product to one of lower quality (and lower price). "Sorting" refers to the cost of getting a bad product off the production line and into quarantine. Unpaid invoices include those costs that will never be paid because of irate customers, and those invoices whose payment is delayed and

Figure 9.2—Cost of quality factors by category

COQ category	Cost factor
Failure	Scrap, rework, regrade, labor, sorting, downtime, slowdowns, complaints, recall, investigations, travel, unpaid invoices, lost sales
Appraisal	Receiving, in-process, final inspection, special tests, test equipment, test technicians, lab maintenance, QC overhead, audits
Prevention	Quality planning, design tolerances, training, housekeeping, packaging, special sourcing, life cycle tests, field tests, shelf tests, pre-production tests, inventories, cash flow

therefore interest is lost. Lost sales may be difficult to estimate, but it's nevertheless a cost of quality, usually attributable to failure of product or service with attendant customer loss.

In the category of appraisal, some of the factors are familiar. In addition to the customary three phases of inspection and test—receiving, in-process, and final—there are quite often special tests that must be arranged. Audits, too, are an appraisal factor and include product, process, and systemwide audits. Some of the factors are continuous whether you're doing an appraisal or not. For example, lab equipment must be purchased and maintained. In addition, there's the higher cost of a staff of test technicians who generally have unique skills appropriate to special test equipment and who require frequent upgrade training.

In ISO 9001, prevention is regarded as equally important to correction. Yet, preventive actions are difficult to verify. Suppose, for example, that you get a flu vaccine and subsequently get through the flu season unscathed. Did the flu shot protect you, or did you benefit from the statistical behavior of the virus? So it is with preventive measures of any kind. Nevertheless, there are recognized steps that can be taken to prevent defective results, and many of them are shown in figure 9.2. Reliability testing is a case in point. The objective of life-cycle tests, field tests, pre-production tests, and shelf tests is to contribute knowledge toward improved design and planning. Design tolerances are preventive because they widen the range of acceptability.

INVENTORY

Inventory is listed in figure 9.2 as a preventive cost of quality. At first glance, the connection between inventory and quality may not be clear, so it's worthwhile to clarify the issue. Richard B. Chase and Nicholas J. Aquilano define inventory in this way: "In manufacturing, inventory refers to inanimate physical entities that contribute to a firm's product output. In services, inventory refers to the productive components necessary to administer the service."[3] Examples of the first kind are raw materials, component parts, and work in process. Examples of service inventory are physical space, number of workstations, productive equipment, and supplies. The purposes of inventory are to maintain an operation independent of supply; to meet variation in demand, to provide flexibility in scheduling; and to take advantage of economic purchase order sizes.

The focus so far has been on production, but where does quality fit in? Japanese manufacturers were the first to see the connection, demonstrating it with the famous "river and rocks" metaphor used by Yoshiki Yamasaki.[4] Imagine a river of just sufficient depth that you can't see the jagged rocks below, capable of destroying your craft. Inventory does the same thing. The more inventory you have, the easier it is to persuade yourself to draw from it to cover losses due to defective material, inefficient machines and workers, and poor management practices. But the losses are still there. The Japanese solution is to use just-in-time strategies in production and inventory. Just-in-time requires greater control of suppliers than has proven practical in a nation as large as the United States, and relatively few companies have succeeded with it. But if just-in-time inventory is superior to massive inventory, it would seem likely that there's a scale of efficiency between the two extremes. It's most important to realize that the connection between inventory and quality is inverse—the lower the inventory, the better the quality.

Inventory can be justified as a preventive factor only if management is aware of its use as compensation for poor quality and is taking remedial steps to remove the cause. In doing so, it remains a cost because both the replacement and the defect have a price and should be noted so that an accurate assignment of cost of quality can be made. This is necessary because the relation of inventory to quality is proportional but not one-to-one. For example, an inventory with a value of $1 million can be used to mask a variable cost of quality.

Inventories tie up cash. Moreover, in-process inventory slows down production. Thus, inventory is a quality consideration from either point of view, which is why the ideal position from the Japanese viewpoint is a just-in-time system. Cash required for operations gets tied up in the interval between investment and revenue derived from sales. Inventory increases this interval, as does poor production. Poor quality in production leads to slowdowns, which reduce cash flow. Thus, cash flow is a quality indicator as well.

FINANCIAL MEASURES

All of the cost factors of figure 9.2 can be translated into the concerns of SOX relative to controls, information, and risk management. However, this isn't particularly useful. At this point, it's sufficient to observe the range and type of costs that permeate the company. Many of them exist as the cost of poor quality, although many exist to prevent it. However, the very diversity of costs challenges the understanding and decision making of executive management. There are literally dozens of metrics to be considered, and it's difficult to weigh their relative importance.

Costs of quality are sometimes called "financial measures of quality." I prefer "financial measures" to "costs of quality" because the former emphasizes the connection of quality to SOX. However, it should be carried one step further. Financial measures of quality should be expressed in terms of the company's strategic objectives and shareholder value. For example:

1. Net income includes net sales minus operating expenses.
2. Operating expenses include cost-of-quality factors.
3. Total assets include accounts receivable plus *all* inventory.
4. Return on total assets is the ratio of net income to total assets.
5. Net income affects the company's market value.

Beginning and ending with net income, the loop of financial measures is closed, tying them all, including quality, to net income. Quality affects the return on assets in two ways because it appears in the numerator as an operating expense and in the denominator as inventory. This is all the more important because return on assets is a measure of profitability and relates directly to the company's strategic goals. But it's item five that will most quickly catch the attention of SOX auditors. A misstatement here can bring serious charges and possible prison time for CEOs. Quality falls under the purview of SOX when the costs of quality—operating costs and inventory—are material. Materiality, in turn, is "auditor-speak" for financial significance and is most visible when financial measures of quality are expressed in terms of profitability and market value.

Therefore, I recommend that "financial measures of quality" refer expressly to costs of quality in terms of profitability and market value. Working with the production manager and chief financial officer, the quality manager can help identify the costs and translate them to financial terms. This will help to keep the company in conformance to SOX and at the same time give quality a preeminence it has been lacking for a long time.

On a final note, a company with a very low defect rate may decide that its cost of quality isn't material. However, if that company is ISO 9001-certified and wins, say, a bid of $1 million on the basis of its certification, then its cost of quality is instantly material.

THE STRATEGIC COST OF QUALITY

The words of SOX are often taken literally. But the directions are flexible and will be flexed by those who see the need to improve quality through the force of liability.

My thesis is that the cost of quality is material to the financial worth of the company and therefore falls under the purview of SOX. How do I arrive at this view? Because when a buyer stipulates that all bidders be ISO 9001-certified, it's requiring a specific quality system as assurance that the performer has the ability to meet customer requirements. Thus, the customer not only pays for the purchased products but also for the quality system itself. This fact can be easily demonstrated by considering the unit cost of production. All corporate costs are included: fixed costs, variable costs, capitalization, and so on. The sum total of these costs is prorated over the number of units purchased by customers, which offers economies of scale. This idea keeps entirely within the view of British Standard 4778 quoted earlier.

Therefore, the customer pays for the entire production system, prorated, in force during the period of performance and for all corporate costs embedded in the cost per unit. It follows that if a customer makes a large purchase, the cost may be material to the financial condition of the company, bringing the transaction under the purview of SOX.

REFERENCES

1. Collins, James C., and Jerry I. Porras. *Built to Last: Successful Habits of Visionary Companies.* New York: Harper Business, 1994.
2. Juran, Joseph M., and Frank Gryna Jr. *Quality Planning and Analysis.* New York: McGraw-Hill, 1980.
3. Chase, Richard B., and Nicholas J. Aquilano. *Production and Operations Management.* Homewood, IL: Richard D. Irwin, 1977.
4. Freeland, James R. "Fundamentals of Just-in-Time." *Colgate Darden Graduate School of Business Administration*, University of Virginia, Sept. 1991.

CHAPTER 10

SOX APPLIED TO ISO 9001

An obvious and perhaps naive conclusion is that the Sarbanes-Oxley Act of 2002 (SOX) applies only to the financial controls of public companies. Corporate organizations today are much too complex to assume that clear-cut divisions of responsibility can be identified. Operations interact, and every activity has a cost that may affect the market value of the company itself. This value can't be misstated upon pain of prosecution under the law.

The prudent CEO, understanding that SOX will require at least a minimum restructure of the way the corporation does business, will capitalize on the opportunity to review the company's total operational picture. It's an occasion to reassess the cohesiveness of management and to integrate and centralize control. The only requirement is that each title of SOX be analyzed for both its stated and potential application, as well as its general utility to central management.

This analysis is predictive but offers important advantages. The advantages of such prediction and potential application are pointed out in this chapter. Chap-

88   ISO 9001 and Sarbanes-Oxley: A System of Governance

ter 8 showed how the ISO 9001 framework could be used to implement SOX requirements because it provides an outline of responsibilities that can be used for guidance and verification, as well as a central source of reference. But this chapter is the most important in the book. It follows the law to its logical conclusion and ties it to quality, thereby putting quality in the forefront. Nothing gains the interest of CEOs more quickly than the realization that they can go to prison for bad quality, if that quality is material to company value.

Most of the titles of SOX can apply to ISO 9001 in some sense. In several of the titles, ISO 9001 is already in compliance with SOX because it performs an equivalent function. That is, if you imagine that title would extend to ISO 9001

Figure 10.1—Correspondences of the Sarbanes-Oxley Act and ISO 9001

SOX Title I—Public Company Accounting Oversight Board
- *ISO 9001 equivalent:* ANSI-ASQ National Accreditation Board (ANAB)
- *ISO 9001 application:* In compliance
- *Duties:* Administer accreditation program

SOX Title II—Auditor independence
- *ISO 9001 equivalent:* ANAB
- *ISO 9001 application:* Near compliance
- *Duties:* Define audit rules

SOX Title III—Corporate responsibility
- *ISO 9000 equivalent:* Management review (5.6.2)
- *ISO 9001 application:* Company executive audit committee
- *Duties:*
  - Certify and audit report as true
  - Respect auditor independence
  - Certify compliance (4.2.2)

SOX Title IV—Enhanced financial disclosures
- *ISO 9000 equivalent:* None
- *ISO 9001 application:* Management responsibility: QMS conformance
- *Duties:*
  - Certify internal controls (4.1), effectively certifying conformance
  - Code of ethics
  - Openness to customers (4.1; 7.1)

SOX Title V—Analyst conflicts of interest
- *ISO 9000 equivalent:* Customer focus (5.2)
- *ISO 9001 application:* In compliance
- *Duties:* Put customer interests first (5.2; 7.2)

Figure 10.1—Correspondences of the Sarbanes-Oxley Act and ISO 9001 (continued)

SOX Title VI—Commission resources and authority
- *ISO 9000 equivalent:* ANAB
- *ISO 9001 application:* In compliance
- *Duties:* Set professional standards

SOX Title VII—Studies and reports
- *ISO 9000 equivalent:* ANAB
- *ISO 9001 application:* In compliance
- *Duties:* Regulate registrars and standards

SOX Title VIII—Corporate and criminal fraud accountability
- *ISO 9000 equivalent:* None
- *ISO 9001 application:* Management responsibility: records/documents
- *Duties:*
  - Retain accurate records (4.2; 8.0)
  - Protect employees

SOX Title IX—White-collar crime penalty enhancements
- *ISO 9000 equivalent:* None
- *ISO 9001 application:* Management responsibility: reports/documents
- *Duties:* Retain accurate reports (4.2; 8.0)

SOX Title X—Corporate tax returns
- *ISO 9000 equivalent:* None
- *ISO 9001 application:* None
- *Duties:* None

SOX Title XI—Corporate fraud accountability
- *ISO 9000 equivalent:* None
- *ISO 9001 application:* Management responsibility: records/documents
- *Duties:* Retain accurate records (4.2; 8.0)
  (Criminal penalties for false reports needed in legal proceedings)

---

by imposing an equivalent requirement, then you'll find that ISO 9001 already invokes that requirement. With respect to other titles, there's a direct application in the meaning or the spirit of the law. Titles III, IV, and VIII can have significant effect in quality. Figure 10.1 provides a brief summary of the correspondence of SOX and ISO 9001.

This chapter closely examines each SOX title for its equivalence or applicability to ISO 9001. Each examination also includes a brief review of section requirements from chapter 6, sparing the need to flip back through the book.

TITLE I: PUBLIC COMPANY ACCOUNTING OVERSIGHT BOARD

Section 101 establishes the Public Company Accounting Oversight Board (PCAOB), with responsibility to oversee the audit of public companies subject to the securities laws. The PCAOB registers public accounting firms that prepare audit reports for public companies, establishes rules for financial audits, ethics, and auditor independence, conducts inspections of registered public accounting firms, conducts investigations and disciplinary proceedings, and enforces compliance with SOX. Thus, the PCAOB is designed to "regulate the regulators." It applies to accounting firms and not to public companies, per se.

Just as the PCAOB administers the financial audit of public companies, an equivalent board under ISO 9001 would administer the quality audit of public companies. Such a board exists: the American National Standards Institute-American Society for Quality National Accreditation Board (ANAB).

The ANAB is the U.S. accreditation body for management systems and accredits certification bodies (also known as registrars) for ISO 9001 quality management systems, ISO 14001 environmental management systems, as well as a number of industry-specific requirements. The certification bodies, in turn, are authorized to certify the management systems of public and private companies in regard to their compliance and conformance to quality and environmental standards. They do this through periodic third-party auditor verification. It should be noted that, as with the PCAOB, the ANAB is designed to regulate the regulators. Its rules apply to certification bodies and not directly to companies in the marketplace.

A manufacturer or service provider is free either to apply for ISO 9001 certification or not, which is what distinguishes the ANAB from the PCAOB. On one hand, companies subject to the rules of the Securities and Exchange Commission must utilize financial accounting firms that are certified by the PCAOB—they must obey the law. On the other hand, no company is forced to obtain ISO 9001 certification. However, it's often true that certification to ISO 9001 is a bidding requirement, and companies pursuing such contracts have little choice in the marketplace. In addition, such certification does establish a level of competence and is itself a marketable commodity.

The ANAB, which is headquartered in Milwaukee, Wisconsin, is a not-for-profit organization that's financially self-supported and governed by a board of directors representing stakeholders. Policy is established by the ANAB board of directors. ANAB exists to serve the conformity assessment needs of business and industry. Because the ANAB is parallel to the PCAOB, ISO 9001 can already be considered compliant to title I. The first step is taken in the integration of ISO 9001 and SOX.

TITLE II: AUDITOR INDEPENDENCE

Nowhere do SOX and ISO 9001 have greater similarity than in title II. Both programs are heavily reliant on auditing—both third-party and internal—SOX for financial controls and ISO 9001 for quality controls. Third-party audits are those in which an external and independent auditing company performs the audit of a client company, usually to verify and validate its compliance to a standard, with the objective being to achieve or maintain certification to that standard. Internal audits are those performed by an audit team composed of employees within the client company, usually to verify its conformance to a standard, with the objective of maintaining its credentials in certification, or of preparing for an external audit.

Independence is defined as freedom from bias and external influences.[1] In this case, external doesn't mean external to the client company; it means external to the audit team. For example, suppose that a person is an employee in a company and is subsequently assigned to an internal audit team. Now suppose that a manager attempts to influence the evaluations or conclusions of the auditor, where the manager might be from the audited process, auditing department, or the employee's own assigned department. In this case, all personnel actions are internal because all persons are employees within the client company. And yet, they're all external interferences. The audit team, led by an experienced team leader, can discuss, dispute, and negotiate to arrive at clear findings and a cohesive report. No one else should interfere.

Bias is the bane of auditing and can come from a variety of sources. It can be called an undue internal influence because if it exists, it lies within the mind of the auditor. The bias could be against the process, process owner, process operator, or for one reason or another, the client company itself. Any judgment arrived at under any influence other than the objective evidence is a biased judgment. Biased audits are invalid, but they're not always evident. There are two kinds: Type I would be an adverse conclusion, whereas the process itself works fine. This kind of conclusion would be contested by the audited process owner and so is the easiest bias to detect. A type II-biased audit would be a favorable conclusion, whereas the process itself is ineffective. This kind of conclusion wouldn't likely be contested by the audited process owner and so is the most difficult bias to detect.

In light of these notions about auditor independence, let's examine the criteria of title II to see their applicability to both SOX and ISO 9001, and to anticipate the integration of the two standards. In brief, section 201 prohibits an audit firm from performing a nonaudit service to an "issuer" (i.e., client company) contemporaneously. Section 203 rotates the lead auditor every five years. Section 204 requires the audit team to report its rules and procedures to the issuer audit committee. Section 206 deals with conflict of interest between the audit firm and the issuer company. Section 207 rotates the audit firms certifying an issuer. Section 209 empowers state regulators to determine if the board's requirements are applicable to companies of all sizes.

Let's consider the most difficult section first—section 201. Chapter 6 explains why it's a bad idea for a company to provide consulting and auditing services to the same client in the same matter. You can't consult and advise a client company on how to structure a process, and then come in as an auditor and claim objectivity in evaluating the process. It's your process. Yet, the ANAB has accepted this arrangement until quite recently.

But it was not always so. When ISO 9001 first hit America's shores in 1987, the dual service of consulting and auditing weren't considered ethical. Generally, small entrepreneurs provided consulting services, while large companies served as registrars and performed the certifying audits. The two never mixed. At some point during the mid-1990s, it became apparent to the registrars that there was a lot of money to be made in consulting, so they began to offer those services too. The Registrar Accreditation Board (RAB), which accredited the registrars in those days, closed its eyes. Companies seeking certification quickly saw the benefit in hiring the same company to perform both services, and the small consultancy business dried up.

Recently, the ANAB has moved to invoke conflict-of-interest restrictions on consulting and auditing. A newly revised Advisory 16, incumbent on certification bodies, requires a two-year interval between consulting and auditing the same client company. This is a step in the right direction, but it isn't clear whether it meets the strict criteria of SOX. Until the major certification bodies recognize the ethical issues involved in the matter of both consulting and evaluating your own work, ISO 9001 will not be in compliance to SOX or to any other ethical standard. Chapter 1 discusses the search for a balance between individual rights and society's rights, and how that often spills over into business.

This balance can be difficult to resolve. In the case of consulting and auditing, there are numerous rights to consider. There are the many small entrepreneurs providing counsel without the capacity for providing certification. There are the few major companies providing certification that are also able to add the efficiency of providing counsel. The client companies looking to minimize cost, and society requiring quality, integrity, and affordability must be considered as well. With respect to ISO 9001, the big auditors carried the day and won the right to consult; however in doing so, society lost out because quality isn't served in this arrangement.

Auditor independence comes down to ensuring objectivity of judgment. This assurance is improved by either eliminating or reducing the occasions that can corrupt or confuse objectivity. For example, section 203 requires the audit firm to periodically rotate its lead auditor vis-à-vis a client company. The reasoning here is clear. After the hard work of the audit itself, and before an audit assessment is given, the audit team gets together to compare notes and determine the findings, if any. Other auditors on the team will generally have less experience than the lead auditor and may require some advice, clarification, or direction. In every case the lead auditor is responsible for audit results and has great influence in the wording of the audit report.

The client company is aware of the authority of the lead auditor and, over the years, may choose to cultivate a relationship that will compromise objectivity. Even if this isn't the case, as people get to know each other well, an amity (or enmity) is established between them.

Finally, objectivity is reduced by one of the characteristics of auditing—familiarity. We often ask ourselves, "How is it that a consultant can go into a company and point out a problem the company itself couldn't see?" This happens all the time and is the basis for consulting. The fact is, when we're familiar with a process, we tend to see how it ought to work rather than how it really does work. That's why audit teams are effective. Auditors are never as familiar with a process as are the process owners and operators—indeed, audit ethics prohibit an auditor from auditing his or her own process. The unfamiliarity of the auditor with the process being audited forces the auditor to "go by the book," and thus see what's really happening rather than what ought to be happening.

Therefore, rotating the lead auditor from time to time serves to improve the objectivity of the audit by reducing the effect of familiarity on the most influential member of the audit team. This rule is just as important in a quality audit as in a financial audit, and such policy is within the purview of the ANAB.

Section 204 requires the audit team to report its rules and procedures to the company audit committee. It might not be clear at first what this has to do with auditor independence. The law is effective in two ways. Understanding the rules and procedures of the audit enables the client company's management to know in advance what to expect, and to know what constraints and limitations are placed upon it in their approach to the audit team. The same can be said from the other direction—the audit team knows in advance what to expect, and what constraints and limitations are placed upon it in its approach to the company. If the rules and procedures are well written, there's minimal opportunity for digression from the strict objectives of the audit, and unfertile ground for familiarity or undue influence.

Again, the policy of section 204 is completely applicable to quality auditing and is within the purview of the ANAB. However, there's a slight but important difference in the organization of the two standards. SOX requires a public company to name an audit committee, which must be composed of top management. ISO 9001 has no such requirement, although clause 5.6 does require management review of audit results.

There are ISO 9001-certified companies that assign the review of audit results to the quality manager under the assumption that, because that person has a direct line to the CEO, the quality management review meets the requirement of ISO 9001. It may meet the requirement, but it doesn't meet the intention. The intention of clause 5.6 is that top management conduct the review of audit results; that way it's done by a board with a wide range of expertise. There are companies that do it this way, such as Metro Machine Corp. of Chesapeake, Virginia.[2] The confusion can be cleared up and the intent of SOX achieved by a cooperative effort between two principal players: the ANAB and ISO Technical Committee 176, which are responsible for the ISO 9000 standard series.

Section 206 restrains conflict of interest by prohibiting an audit firm's former employees from serving in the top-management level of a client company. The prohibition makes sense, which became clear in the Enron aftermath. If an audit firm doesn't detect "cooked books," they may not be detected at all, and a former employee could be in a position to influence the audit. This situation is also possible in a third-party quality audit because even though we don't often think of the monetary value of ISO 9001 certification, it's very real. A large market is open to those who are ISO 9001-certified and is closed to those who aren't. ANAB has the authority to establish a policy similar to that of section 206. This would be a rule, not of ISO 9001 per se, but of achieving certification itself.

Section 207 rotates the audit firms that certify the financial reports of a client company. The same argument applies here as applied in the rotation of lead auditors—the avoidance or reduction of familiarity. The mandatory rotation of accreditors is important in the world of quality. For one thing, client companies tend to cluster into given industries. Whether their financial books are similar, their production and service processes aren't, and an accrediting company must have the expertise to conduct specific audits. So although there are many accrediting companies, there may be relatively few with competence in a given industry. And like everything, the less competition there is, the higher the cost.

As discussed in chapter 6, the Comptroller General has postponed a decision on the matter of section 207 until the trade-off in risks and benefits can be more firmly established. There's little motivation for ANAB to tackle this perplexing problem any further than the government has. Although it has yet to be proven that the existing system of long-term relationships is harmful to the world of finance, much less quality, the dispute goes on. Further scandal will bring the issue back to center stage.

To sum up, ISO 9001 is almost in compliance with title II because ANAB is empowered to define audit rules and duplicate applicable sections. Yet, there's a gigantic hurdle that ANAB must get over if ISO 9001 is to be compliant: Certifying bodies must have their right to consult client companies withdrawn. So ISO 9001 is near, but not in, compliance with title II.

TITLE III: CORPORATE RESPONSIBILITY

This title could have a significant effect on ISO 9001 due to its requirement for certification, and calls for a brief review. Recall that under section 204, the audit firm had to report its rules and procedures to the issuer audit committee that's presumed to exist. Section 301 ensures that such a committee does indeed exist by requiring the client company to establish one. This audit committee must be an independent, executive management body. Section 302 requires certification of the audit report as true by the CEO and CFO. Section 303 prohibits executive management from improper influence of an auditor in a financial audit report.

Applied to ISO 9001's clause 5.1, section 301 would create an executive management audit committee with responsibility for the outcome of an ISO 9001 audit. This function already exists under the internal audit requirements of clause 8.2.2 and the management review of clause 5.1.

Section 303 requires respect for auditor independence, which would apply to third-party auditors. (It's self-defeating to ignore internal auditors, but a company is under no obligation to follow their recommendations.) A company might challenge the external audit—in quality audits this happens quite often—but it couldn't improperly influence the auditors in their findings. By "challenge," I mean that the company might question the correctness of auditor observations or conclusions, and reasoned arguments and negotiations might follow. Section 303 is a fundamental audit policy and is just as reasonable in a quality audit as in a financial one.

Section 302 has a huge potential effect on quality because it requires the CEO and CFO to certify a financial report. Is there an ISO 9001 equivalent? The closest thing quality has to a financial report is its quality manual, which isn't much of a stretch when you think about it. The financial report attests to the health of the company's finances and compliance to SOX. The quality manual is essentially a report of the company's quality management system (QMS). It attests to the health of the company's QMS and compliance with ISO 9001. It has monetary value, too, because it can be the basis of winning a bid. If you win a bid because you're ISO 9001-certified but your quality manual isn't in compliance, it's possible fraud. Therefore, a SOX-based ISO 9001 system would require the CEO to certify compliance of the company's quality manual to ISO 9001.

One could argue that ISO 9001 compliance is already certified by a certifying body. Yet, the same argument could be made, and has been made, in the financial world prior to SOX. In the past, a public accounting firm would come in and certify the company books as compliant with SEC rules. Under SOX, a company can no longer use this argument. Yes, the accounting firm verifies the books, but the CEO and CFO certify them. An ISO 9001 registrar will also come in and verify compliance and conformance of a company's QMS, but if section 302 were to be applied to ISO 9001 clause 5.6.1, the CEO would have to certify the QMS as being in compliance.

What's to be gained by applying section 302 to quality? Suppose that the registrar and the company are in collusion. Or suppose the registrar is too lenient. If a customer believes itself the victim of a performer in noncompliance, it doesn't want to pursue the registrar; it wants to go after the performer. By requiring the CEO to attest to compliance of the quality manual, SOX would hold the performer, not the registrar, responsible for compliance.

TITLE IV: ENHANCED FINANCIAL DISCLOSURES

Title IV also has the potential for a significant effect on ISO 9001. Although it's not one of the certifying sections of SOX, if applied to ISO 9001 it could call for certification of internal controls. Let's review the requirements to see how this interpretation makes sense.

Section 404 requires top management to assess whether an internal control is working properly. It's up to management to determine which controls it wants to monitor. Management is responsible for them all. As an example of the potential size of the task, consider the company information system. Some observers, such as Gary Bolles, recognize that this system falls under the purview of SOX because financial matters are retained here.[3] The PCAOB also sees a vital connection, saying, "The nature and characteristics of a company's use of information technology in its information system affect the company's internal control over financial reporting."[4]

Chapter 6 stated that the standard for information technology (IT), Control Objectives for Information Technology, calls for thirty-four internal controls. It's apparent that under SOX, top management has a new and major task to add to its already full plate. In addition to finance, it's responsible for IT controls, too. Quality systems also have controls, although calling them that has dropped out of favor. For example, a measurement is a control. It tells you whether an attribute or value is acceptable. Sometimes a signature is a control. There are literally dozens of controls in quality, depending on how you count them.

Applied to ISO 9001 clause 4.1c, section 404 would assign responsibility of process controls to top management. Is this an outrageous demand on top management? Well, Japanese managers do it all the time. Masaaki Imai exhorts all managers, "Go to Gemba! Go to the workplace and see what's going on!"[5] SOX tells top management: "You're responsible for how well your processes work." Managing internal controls is like managing anything else. You must study the totality of the picture and determine those key events that indicate the state of things. In doing so, you learn how the larger system works. This is the intent of SOX, and it's what Imai had in mind with his exhortation.

Section 406 requires a code of ethics for financial officers. The nearest that ISO 9000 gets to this is ISO 9004 clause 5.1.1, which isn't contractual. Chapter 6 argues that a code of ethics is an intrinsic part of professionalism. The requirement for a code of managerial ethics is within the purview of ISO 9001 clause 5.0. A viable code is presented in detail in chapter 2.[6]

Section 409 requires real-time disclosure of material changes in the financial condition or operations of the issuer. Chapter 6 discusses an ambiguity in the wording and concluded that no matter the interpretation, the changes might influence market price, and so are subject to SOX scrutiny. Material operational changes might also affect contract performance and should be disclosed to the customer in real time. Applied to ISO 9001 clauses 4.1.f or 7.1.f, section 409 would provide visibility to customers and shareholders.

The most critical section of title IV is section 404, which requires an issuer to state the responsibility of top management for maintaining an adequate internal control structure, and to assess its effectiveness. In fact, the section doesn't require top managers to certify their system of internal controls, but it does require them to attest to its effectiveness. We can't expect ISO 9001 to be stricter than SOX, but the phrase "and attest to its effectiveness" could be added to clause 4.1(c). In sum, title IV would pair with title III. Title III would require a CEO to certify compliance of the quality manual; title IV would require a CEO to attest to controls and, hence, to conformance of the quality system.

TITLE V: ANALYST CONFLICTS OF INTEREST

Section 501 requires rules that would prevent analysts from making recommendations in their own interests and not in that of the investor. At first glance, there's little direct application to ISO 9001. The only buying and selling going on is between the registrar and client company, and conflicts of interest in this area would come under title II—auditor independence.

Like everything else about SOX, one must examine the principles involved. Conflict of interest isn't the principle here—customer interests are. The prohibition on conflict of interest is made by SOX to protect the customer. Stated this way, title V does indeed have application to ISO 9001. Applied to ISO 9001, clause 7.2, section 501 would put customer interests first. However, these interests are already required in ISO 9001:2000, under customer focus. Therefore, ISO 9001 is already in compliance with title V.

TITLE VI: COMMISSION RESOURCES AND AUTHORITY

By "commission," title VI is referring to the SEC. Section 601 authorizes appropriations; the remaining sections discuss its authority. Applied to ISO 9001, title VI would refer to the ANAB. This organization is already funded for its role and has the authority to set professional standards. Therefore, ISO 9001 is already in compliance with title VI.

TITLE VII: STUDIES AND REPORTS

The "studies and reports" referred to in title VII concern the request to the Comptroller General to study the regulation of public accounting and investment firms. A similar requirement in ISO 9001 would refer to registrars. Therefore, title VII would apply to the ANAB, which already has the authority to regulate registrars and standards. Therefore, ISO 9001 is already in compliance with title VII.

TITLE VIII: CORPORATE AND CRIMINAL FRAUD ACCOUNTABILITY

Title VIII applies to both public and private companies.[7] Section 802 makes it a felony to knowingly destroy or create documents to impede, obstruct, or influence an existing or contemplated federal investigation. It defines the retention of records, and provides criminal penalties. Section 806 also provides whistleblowing protection, prohibits threats and harassment against employees, and defines compensatory damages.

Although title VIII only specifically addresses the financial function of a company, its relevance to manufacturing and service is clear and immediate. Chapter 5 lists various kinds of records that are used in the manufacturing cycle. In some companies these records are destroyed or altered on occasion to meet contract requirements or to realize a profit.

The argument can be made that altering such records has financial consequences, and one might assume the action will be revealed in examining the financial books. Not necessarily. In principle, fraudulent actions on the factory floor or at the service counter do spill over into the financial arena—making money is usually the objective of fraud. However, the evidence lies in the nature of the doctored documents, and they're out on the floor of operations, not in the counting room. In this sense, fraud or false claims related to operations is in the direct purview of both SOX and quality. Although it's true that the scandals leading to the creation of SOX were straightforward theft, money is also lost through fraud on the production line. This affects the true shareholder value of the company. Any kind of fraud that affects the market value of a company is the business of SOX.

In the 19 months between its creation in July of 2002, to February of 2004, the President's Corporate Fraud Task Force has brought significant criminal charges against 87 corporations.[8] The list includes the dozen or so companies charged as a result of the financial scandals that followed the Enron explosion, but the crimes of the remainder cover the spectrum of malfeasance. Assuming that all 87 cases affected the market value of their companies, SOX would have applied to them had it been enacted sooner. It applies now.

Applied to ISO 9001 clauses 4.2.3, 4.2.4, and 8.0, title VIII would encourage honesty in records, empower employees, and enhance pride of workmanship. It encourages honest records by making their alteration a criminal offense if the intent of the alteration is in violation of SOX criteria. There's a double risk to the miscreant if that person is a manager who pressures a subordinate to doctor records because then *two* people know about it. The employee may alter a record for self-advantage—say, to make individual performance look good. But more often than not, the alteration of documentation occurs because employees are instructed by superiors to "fudge the numbers" for purposes of increasing production, which is a management goal.

Title VIII empowers employees by protecting them from fear, from being forced to do bad work, and from retaliation. Consider a situation in which an employee is told to cover up a defect in a piece of work, or to change the result of a test. Say a nondestructive test is being run in which the depth of a drilled hole must not exceed a tolerance, but in fact it does. A supervisor instructs the employee to pass the test. This is disempowerment because it strips the employee of decision-making authority relative to his or her own work. In chapter 2, I quoted military standard 9858A: "Personnel who perform quality functions shall have sufficient, well-defined responsibility, authority, and *organizational freedom* to identify and evaluate quality problems and to initiate, recommend, or provide solutions." This requirement was placed in the standard precisely to prevent managerial overrule and enhance empowerment.

If an employee insists on doing good work even though it slows production, or if the employee blows the whistle on what appears to be a product or service that's unworthy of the customer it's being delivered to, there's a certain probability of retaliation by management. To prevent or reduce retaliation, title VIII spells it out: "No company, or any officer, employee, contractor, subcontractor, or agent of such company may discharge, demote, suspend, threaten, harass, or in any other manner discriminate against an employee in the terms and conditions of employment because of any lawful act done by the employee...."

ISO 9001 doesn't directly address the issue of employee protection against management use of fear, coercion, abuse, or retaliation. It's as though these issues are so heinous they perish the thought. You can get there after a fashion. For example, clause 6.4 says, "The organization shall determine and manage the work environment needed to achieve conformity to product requirements." This also applies to service requirements. Now, clause 6.4 is in the form of a finding. If a company is systemic in turning out defective work, you can take clause 6.4 and work back, possibly connecting the finding to causes in the work environment. However, being in uncharted waters, one can stray elsewhere. Indeed, the miscreant will also work back, find a different path that defends the slovenly work, and claim that you've failed to establish cause and effect.

It's pointed out in chapter 2 that the Mil-Q-9858A standard provided employees with the authority to evaluate their own work. One of the first things some supervisors will do if production falls behind schedule is strip employees of this authority and retaliate if they complain. Title VIII provides protection to employees who insist on doing good work.

TITLE IX: WHITE-COLLAR CRIME PENALTY ENHANCEMENTS

Section 906 requires that each periodic report containing financial statements filed pursuant to the Securities and Exchange Act of 1934 be accompanied by a certification of the CEO and CFO that the report fully complies with, and fairly represents in all material respects, the financial condition and results of operations of the company. To repeat an important point from chapter 6, section 906 differs from section 302 in that its certification is absolute, with no qualifier.[9] Section 906 defines fraudulent accountability as a crime.

As with each title of SOX, one must consider the intent of the law to see its potential application to ISO 9001. The intent of title IX is to ensure the financial statements that may accompany reports are true. The equivalent reports in quality might be test reports or reports attesting to the effectiveness of a quality process or of the quality system. Test reports are statements of value delivered. Reports about the efficacy of processes or systems may be statements of a priori or a posteriori value, used either to obtain a contract or in pursuit of payment on a contract. If the reports are false, the customer is cheated of value whether or not the executive management of the performing company knew of the falsehoods. If a version of section 906 were applied to clauses 4.2.3, 4.2.4, or 8.0 of ISO 9001, it could criminalize the dishonest reports and fraudulent quality systems that had material monetary effect on the contract.

Combined with other SOX applications to ISO 9001, one might wonder if top management is being overanalyzed in regard to production or service—creating too great a burden of suspicion. After all, dishonesty in the workplace isn't as bad as dishonesty in accounting, is it? Surely, absconding with $40 million is far worse than cheating on the report of, say, a valve test. But if the valve test has a material effect on the cost of quality, and we're talking about hundreds of thousands of valves, well, yes, dishonesty in the workplace may well be as bad as dishonesty in the accounting room.

TITLE X: CORPORATE TAX RETURNS

This title requires the CEO to sign the corporate income tax return. There's no apparent connection of title X to ISO 9001.

TITLE XI: CORPORATE FRAUD AND ACCOUNTABILITY

Section 1102 is similar in intent to title VIII and concerns the destruction of evidence, where the evidence destroyed may have had value in a legal proceeding. So the person intending to defraud again faces a double hazard. In titles VIII and IX it's a crime to create dishonest records and reports; in title XI it's a crime to destroy them.

Applied to ISO 9001 clauses 4.2.3, 4.2.4, and 8.0, this title would criminalize the destruction or alteration of quality records to impair an official proceeding. The same argument applies here as in title VIII and IX: Dishonesty in production or service is a cost to the customers and shareholders and should have consequences for the miscreant.

SOX is about fraud. Resulting from the theft of hundreds of millions of dollars of shareholder value, the law was written to protect investors from deceitful claims of dishonest corporate management. However, the shareholder isn't the only victim of corporate dishonesty. The customer, too, can suffer similar losses through dishonest production and services. There's a similar need for a law that defines specific wrongdoings in the workplace, enables the description of evidence, and improves the understanding of management at all levels of the meaning of ethical behavior and of quality.

REFERENCES

1. Russell, J. P. *The Quality Audit Handbook.* ASQ Quality Audit Division, Milwaukee: ASQ Quality Press, 1997.
2. Stimson, William A. *Metro Machine Corporation: A Malcolm Baldrige Quality Award Assessment.* Systems Engineering Department, School of Engineering and Applied Science, University of Virginia, June 28, 1993.
3. Bolles, Gary A. "Technology: Sarbanes-Oxley." *CIO Insight: Strategies for Business Leaders.* Ziff Davis Media Inc. Aug. 8, 2003.
4. Public Company Accounting Oversight Board. "An Audit of Internal Control Over Financial Reporting Performed in Conjunction with an Audit of Financial Statements." Final Auditing Standard, Release No. 2004–2001, March 9, 2004.
5. Imai, Masaaki. *Gemba Kaizen.* New York: McGraw-Hill, 1997.
6. Stimson, William A. "A Deming-Inspired Management Code of Ethics." *Quality Progress,* Feb. 2005, pp. 67–75.
7. Lieberman, Larry D. "Sarbanes-Oxley Affects Your Private Company Clients." *Wisconsin Lawyer,* Vol. 77, No. 6, June 2004.
8. "Corporate Fraud Task Force Cases and Charging Documents," United States Department of Justice, Feb. 20, 2004, *www.usdoj.gov.*
9. "The Sarbanes-Oxley Act of 2002." Corporate Department, Carter, Ledyard, and Milburn, LLP. July 2002.

CHAPTER 11

CONCLUSIONS AND RECOMMENDATIONS

Taking vigorous steps to restore investor confidence in the U.S. marketplace, Congress passed the Public Company Accounting Reform and Investor Protection Act of 2002. Popularly known as the Sarbanes-Oxley Act (SOX), the law mandates strict requirements for the financial accounting of public companies. SOX focuses on the internal controls of a company's financial system and, in particular, holds top management responsible for the effectiveness and efficiency of these controls. Certain financial reports must be certified as materially correct, and in the event of false claims, penalties are levied against individuals as well as the corporation.

SOX applies not only to a company's financial system, but also to its information system, given that much, if not all, the company's financial reports and controls lie in this system. Thus, the breadth of corporate processes under the purview of SOX is extensive, and a suitable system of governance would be beneficial in providing a unifying structure to SOX requirements.

CONCLUSION ONE: A UNIFIED SYSTEM OF CORPORATE GOVERNANCE

ISO 9001 is a system of governance that integrates all of the processes, functions, and activities of a company into a formal framework. Thus, an existing ISO 9001 structure easily lends itself to integration with a company's financial system. Records, reports, resources, controls, reviews, audit functions, responsibilities, monitoring and measurement—all of the components of the financial system will fit into the documentation and process framework of ISO 9001. Also, as the information technology system is already included in the ISO 9001 framework, a comprehensive and single system of corporate governance is achieved, and SOX compliance is easily demonstrated.

The quality assurance department can help in this integration by joining with the finance department and the information officer in mapping their functions to the ISO 9001 format and quality manual. If the name "quality manual" doesn't sit well with the team, then just call it something else—the governance manual, for example. This title has a prestigious ring to it, and few people would object to being associated with what sounds like a top-management document.

CONCLUSION TWO: A SOX-FRIENDLY QUALITY SYSTEM

Just as SOX makes it necessary for the CEO and CFO to understand the financial condition of the company, a SOX-based ISO 9001 certification would also make it necessary for the CEO or general manager to understand the company quality system. For example, if applied to ISO 9001, title III would require top management to certify compliance of the company's quality manual to ISO 9001, and title IV would hold top management accountable for conformance of the company quality system.

These conclusions are based in part on the estimated potential of SOX relative to operational issues, as well as the information many organizations are moving to get SOX authority imposed on corporate operations. For example, members of the ISO community are working to get some of the SOX principles integrated into ISO 9001.

The need for SOX authority is there from the customers' point of view. ISO 9001 is weak only when top management isn't behind it. Yet, many companies win bids on the strength of their ISO 9001 certifications, so the customer has every right to expect good performance based on an effective and efficient system of production or service. If the customer is dissatisfied with a given contract performance and has evidence of performer failure caused by the lack of compliance or conformance to ISO 9001, there are just grounds for civil complaint. SOX would contribute to fair litigation by formalizing the obligation top management has to its customers, just as it now formalizes the obligation it has to its investors.

FINANCIAL CONDITION OR RESULTS OF OPERATIONS

There's no need for SOX to be rewritten or expanded to apply its rigor to operations of production and service. The purview is already there, established in sections 302 and 401, under the phrase, "financial information must fairly present in all material respects the financial condition and results of operations of the issuer." All that's required to apply SOX to production and service is to use a logical interpretation of what this phrase means. Clearly, "the results of operations," being plural, is distinguished from "financial condition." It's therefore reasonable to interpret this phrase to mean that information must be honestly reported if it concerns the material financial effect of operations.

All operations have a financial effect; the question is if the effect is material. Whether it's production and service costs, or financial reports, one can't know until after the fact. SOX is both preventive and corrective. Yes, you can go to prison if you violate certain provisions, but the law mandates internal financial controls to *prevent* adverse effects on shareholder value. On the other hand, SOX is also corrective because active internal controls provide evidence of abuse, neglect, or mishap, if such is the case. Thus, SOX is dually beneficial to investors. Quality controls are also preventive and corrective. Many of the techniques in the quality toolbox that were discussed briefly in chapter 4 are actions to ensure fault-free performance through good design, or to detect patterns that may appear as a result of wear and tear. Many of ISO 9001's requirements initiate authorizations, reviews, measurements, and records to ensure stability of process. All of these actions are to prevent adverse effects to the customer, and are therefore within both the spirit and intent of SOX. As with financial controls, a side benefit to the customer is that quality controls are corrective, providing evidence of abuse, neglect, or mishap, if such is the case.

To a large degree, the decision on whether a cost is material must be shared with the customer. For example, say I have a contract requiring a performance valued at $30,000, which is my annual income, with a performer that annually grosses $30 million. My contract might not be material in the performer's books, but it is in mine.

RECOMMENDATION ONE: AN ISO 9001 FINANCIAL SYSTEM

In today's dynamic global economy, businesses are organizing as integrated processes to optimize performance and reduce costs. As a result of this integration, it's increasingly difficult to separate the notions of production, service, quality, and market value. They're all responsive to, and accountable for, financial performance. Sooner or later operations will join finance and information technology as a direct concern of SOX.

To anticipate the approaching authority of SOX, the prudent CEO must know what's going on at all levels in the company. There are two simple recommendations that will ensure the CEO this control. The first is to set up a financial accounting system conformable to ISO 9001. This organization will be beneficial by creating a single system of governance and an audit-friendly configuration.

A unified system of governance provides a common vocabulary and measurement system throughout the company. Documentation is similar, controls are similar, and common solutions are easier to see. Common metrics can be found for all departments so that the performances of diverse groups can be compared and effective improvements more easily developed. The tasks of management are uniform throughout the company, following the ISO 9001 process approach.

For example, all functions within the ISO 9001 purview must measure their performance for effectiveness and efficiency. Typical metrics might be "accounts receivable and payable" for accounting, "market share" for marketing, "change orders" for contracts, "quotes-to-bookings ratio" for sales, "damage incidents" for handling and storage, "transportation costs per product" for traffic, and "work-in-process inventory turns" for production. All of these metrics can be translated into terms of productivity and expressed in terms of shareholder value. In this way, all levels of management march to the same drum.

All functions within the ISO 9001 purview must document activities such as plans, risk assessments, records, reports, and procedures. Clause 4.2.1, for example, cites documents needed by the company to ensure effective planning, operation, and control of processes as part of the total documentation of the quality system. Clause 4.2.3 lists steps for document control, and clause 4.2.4 discusses the control of records. These matters apply to finance and information technology, as well as operations. They also serve as a reminder, format mechanism, and unifier of corporate documentation.

All functions within the ISO 9001 purview require an internal audit capability. The audit program of each system in the company will be identical in structure. This includes audit training, planning, schedule, checklist, audits, analysis, records and reports, and follow-up. The structure of every audit will also be identical, and includes purpose, scope, and basis. However, each system and each audit will be unique in its details. For example, the financial checklists will be completely different from both the quality checklists and the IT checklist. The qualifications of the auditors will be different. The purpose, scope, and basis will be different. There's no encroachment from system to system—finance, quality, and IT remain distinct in responsibility, authority, and accountability. But from the perspective of top management, there's only one audit program. It will be defined in clause 8.2.2, and though managed by different managers, all audit subprograms will meet its criteria.

RECOMMENDATION TWO: LEARN YOUR PRODUCTION AND SERVICE PROCESSES

In accordance with SOX, U.S. corporate management must assume the responsibility of compliance to its laws on financial reports and conformance to its requirements on internal controls. Sooner or later, this responsibility will extend to corporate operations to prevent the material digression of costs. If the company is ISO 9001-certified, both jobs get easier. I've already discussed how ISO 9001 can help the financial function comply with SOX. The requirement on conformance of internal controls will demand that top management take direct responsibility.

The solution to direct responsibility for top management may not be easy to implement, but it's easy to understand. Top management must learn about production and service processes, and go to process managers and business unit managers to get satisfactory answers to the following questions:

- What is the objective of this process?
- How do you control it?
- How do you verify effectiveness?
- How do you verify your records?
- How do you verify compliance?
- How does this operation compare to best practices?

The answers to these questions will undoubtedly reflect the bottom-up view of the process owners, but top management will learn much about the processes by translating the answers into the overall strategic picture.

What Is the Objective of This Process?

Imagine yourself as an executive manager posing this question at a circuit assembly station. The operator might answer, "I fasten this transformer and these circuit boards in this box, then it goes to the next station." There may be 40 or 50 such stations in the series, and it would seem a monumental task to master the detail and do an analysis of all the stations. You don't have time for this kind of detail, nor is it necessary to your goal—understanding the tactical role of the assembly stream is. You want to determine the highest level of the overall assembly process that best represents what's going on, how it fits in the tactical picture, and what minimum set of metrics is needed for performance assessment. So you do your walk-through, trying to understand the tactical purpose of the assembly.

The bottom-up answer to the objective of a stamping machine is similar. It adds value to a unit of material, readies it for the next station, and then moves it along. You're told the objective of a particular process but know it to be a subprocess of an overall system. You want to arrive at an efficient and effective way to assess this overall system.

Why not just ask the floor manager? It's the same reason you wouldn't ask the plant manager what the plant does. You must know these things from your own reasoning to have the inner knowledge needed to protect yourself from the charge of neglect if SOX compliance isn't maintained. "Going to gemba" to get the bottom-up view of each process or subprocess, then formulating the information into a tactical understanding of how the process works and how to measure it, is enormously enriching. It will also enable you to test the whole operation with respect to the strategic objectives of the company.

How Do You Control It?

The answer to this question is critical to SOX compliance. To understand the answer of the process owner, you need to know what control means and how it's determined. Every process provides either a product or service, which has a target value. No process is perfect, and every process undergoes variation in what it does. Therefore, no product or service will have exactly the correct target value. There will be deviation about the target value. The process is said to be "in control" when its variation is constrained within acceptable limits. Sometimes the acceptable limits are zero. For example, if the control is an authorizing signature on a change order, then a change order with no signature is unacceptable. In mass production or service, a certain amount of deviation is tolerated out of inevitability. Engineers will determine the acceptable range of deviation.

A process is controlled by first making a measurement. The measurement tells you if the process is "in control," that is, if it's stable. Therefore, when you ask the process owner how a process is controlled, you can expect the answer to include a measurement. You might want to see a record of the measurements. If the measurement shows the process isn't in control, you can expect to hear how that instability is identified and what's being done to bring the process back into control.

A series of subprocesses can yield a long list of controls and metrics, but the task of process assessment is made easier by using the tactic of key indicators. Toyota's TABC plant in Long Beach, California, provides a good example of this idea. The plant makes Tacoma truck bodies and catalytic converters and is expanding its automaking capability. In keeping with the Toyota principle of "go to gemba," management visits the work processes frequently. Each process must have a visual display of its quality progress. TABC management uses few metrics to assess process performance. When a process first goes online, a "direct-run ratio" is computed of the number of defects per lot in the first run. When the process is working well, the metric is changed to an "online repair ratio." A third metric, "equipment down-time ratio," is used to measure the effectiveness of maintenance. So with just a few charts, top management can make a valid assessment of the stability of a process. The way those key indicators are determined is by first having a good understanding of how all the subprocesses fit together in the tactical picture.

Once a process is understood, in cooperation with the process owner, it's relatively easy to determine one or a few key indicators of its performance. This is true because most workstations in a sequence are linear. If one is unstable, the process is unstable. If all are stable, the process is stable. Therefore, you don't need key indicators for all the subprocesses, just for the overall process.

How Do You Verify Effectiveness?

ISO 9000 defines "effectiveness" as the measure of the achievement of planned activities and results. Process effectiveness, then, refers to the ability of a process to provide the output it's designed to provide. If the process is in control, you can count on a stable distribution of its output. There will be a fixed mean value and a variance about that mean value. This says nothing of how effective the output is. The effectiveness of a process is tied to a metric called "capability." The capability of a process is the ratio of its acceptable variation compared to its operational variation.

All products and services have an allowable tolerance about target value that's deemed acceptable for use by the design engineers. This variation is sometimes called "the voice of the customer." All processes suffer variation in their output. This process variation is sometimes called "the voice of the process." Hence, the capability of a process is the ratio of the voice of the customer compared to the voice of the process.

The metric of capability, as defined here, is applicable to every process and activity in a company. This includes production, finance, transportation, and administration. So for every process, the process owner should be able to explain what that capability is and how it's determined.

How Do You Verify Your Records?

Documentation control is one of the required elements of SOX included in its concept of internal controls. The physical control itself is necessary but not sufficient. There must be evidentiary records. One of the advantages of ISO 9001 is that clause 4.2 provides for excellent document control. If you're ISO 9001-certified, you can expect that your process owner has met the requirements of clause 4.2 and can explain to you how they're implemented. If you're not ISO 9001 certified, you must set up some sort of document control system that satisfies SOX and is recognizable or explainable to auditors. An ISO 9001-conformable system fits the bill and is as easy to set up as any other.

How Do You Verify Compliance?

I speak here of compliance to SOX and other applicable laws and regulations, and not to ISO 9001, the latter being determined by registrars. SOX compliance is achieved through internal controls. Your process owner should understand the COSO definition of internal controls well enough to explain how the process achieves compliance. The COSO definition states: "Internal control is a process designed to provide reasonable assurance regarding the achievement of objectives in the following categories: Effectiveness and efficiency of operations, reliability of financial reporting; and Compliance with applicable laws and regulations."[1] Reviewing this definition, you'll note that the first three questions you're asking are framed precisely so that satisfactory answers are sufficient to demonstrate SOX compliance.

How Does This Operation Compare to Best Practices?

Simply complying with the law or a standard of governance such as ISO 9001 won't earn a dime. Processes must not only be effective; they must also be efficient. Your costs are reduced and profits increased through efficiency of operations. Competition in the marketplace always ensures that if there's a better way to do something, someone is either already doing it or knows about it. Your process owner, if a professional person, should be aware of best practices in that process, and where to go to find out about them.

Some best practices are proprietary, and few companies will share their money-making efficiencies with you. Others have been codified into a standard and are available at modest cost. Several of them are identified in this book: ISO 9001 as a best practice for governance; CobIT as a best practice for IT management; and COSO Enterprise Risk Management as a best practice for dealing with risk. For smaller-scale processes, there are a variety of technical manuals, equipment, genre and system publications, professional journals, and commercial notices to stimulate thought on the matter. Your process owner should display awareness of this knowledge base and be able to explain where the process in question fits into the best practices scale. It may be that an upgrade on the existing process is required, or even a new one, and a cost analysis will have to be made. The important point here, if you're to maintain the company in competition, is that the process owner be able to express a learned position on best practices relative to the process.

THE STRATEGIC VIEW

With an understanding of the tactical use of company processes in achieving their purpose in an effective and efficient manner, top management has the knowledge to assess capability in terms of a company's strategic goals. Why is this necessary? Long-term stability comes from closed-loop operation. You determine the mission and strategic objectives of the company and gather resources to achieve them. This motion will go on for several years and take on a life of its own as the organization grows. The question then arises as to whether you can loop back to where you came from. The mission and strategy lead to the organization. Does the organization lead back to the mission and strategic objectives at every level of aggregation?

Kenneth D. MacKenzie shows that the correspondence between line organizations and the strategy that sets them up is less than 50 percent, and that a good one would rate about 60 percent.[2] There are several reasons for this disparity, and they're difficult to detect because they grow slowly. You get used to them and work in compensation for the inefficiencies. Three of the disparities that grow with time are incongruence, interdependence, and inflexibility.

Processes that have similar missions, policies, strategies, and procedures are congruent and can be effectively integrated into a coherent whole. This congruence must be designed into the system and maintained throughout the life cycle of the process. It's not enough to say, "Let there be information technology." The mission, policy, strategy, and procedures of IT must be congruent with production, human resources, operations, and so on, for IT to be fully integrated and coherent to the company mission.

When the need for any kind of resource for one process overlaps with that of another, an interdependence is created that complicates the operation of both and confounds projections. Projections are often calculated from probability distributions, where each process is considered independent. Joint probability distributions are often unknown. Thus, congruence is required in resource management as well as in operations.

It's reasonable to create a process with the primary consideration being what it is that the process is supposed to do. However, from their very concept, processes should be designed to be flexible—particularly for maintenance and updating. An automobile is a simple example of the first, and a personal computer an example of the second. Many automobiles have been designed so that the engine must be removed to gain access to relatively inexpensive parts in need of replacement, but that has nothing to do with the engine block. A computer is kept for a few years and then thrown out for a new one because it can't be upgraded to newly required capabilities. These occasions are frustrating, yet many companies suffer the same inflexibility in their processes because they weren't designed with the future in mind.

In the very distant past, if a person broke an arm in an accident or in battle it mended as well as possible, often causing a crippling condition for the victim. Nature pushes on. Processes do likewise. If there's a shortcoming in the design of a process that limits its ability to perform a task, it will nevertheless make the attempt to meet expectations. One of the compensations that may be used is the "virtual position." This is a function assigned to a process but which has no supervisor-subordinate chain. The task gets done but not according to the chart. It's without funding, recognition, and legitimate resources.

I once witnessed a virtual position on a surface-mount technology assembly line in a telecommunications company. With time and experience, an operator had created, on his own initiative, a control point (i.e., an inspection station). The purpose of this ad hoc inspection was to correct accumulating defects caused by serial dependence before the unit arrived at the regular inspection station. This reduced the official defect rate recorded at the regular station. One can argue about the pros and cons of this strategy, but the ad hoc inspection added one more workstation to the line—though it never appeared on the organization chart.

In preparing for SOX compliance in operations, the second recommendation to executive management is to learn the production and service processes. Realistically, top management must be selective in the detail that can be examined to ensure control. MacKenzie refers to this notion as the "level of aggregation," and it applies to implementing corporate strategy as well as learning how things work. The level of aggregation should be the same for both. You can best determine the strategic congruence of a system of processes at the level you understand them.

SUMMARY

SOX mandates strict requirements for financial accounting of public companies and transforms the public accounting industry. It does this through rules that reform corporate governance through internal controls. Careful reading shows that this governance may well extend to corporate operations, which invariably play a material part in shareholder value.

The implementation of SOX-compliant internal controls within a company immediately applies to corporate finance and information processes. A framework of governance must be built upon, and an existing ISO 9001 structure provides this framework. It easily lends itself to integration with a company's financial system, and quality personnel can provide the expertise to help achieve SOX compliance. At the same time, top management gains a single unifying system of governance over all operations within the company.

It's prudent to anticipate the extension of SOX-compliant internal controls to corporate operations because just as SOX makes it necessary for the CEO to understand the financial condition of the company, he or she must understand the operational processes as well. This is because modern companies are organizing as integrated processes, and it's becoming increasingly difficult to separate the notions of production, service, quality, and market value. Understanding operational processes isn't as difficult as it may seem if the CEO goes about the task judiciously, determining key indicators of the state of the overall systems.

SOX is the handwriting on the wall. It will lead to a new way of doing business, where ethical practice is as important as making money—not just because it's a good idea—but because it's the law.

REFERENCES

1. Committee of Sponsoring Organizations of the Treadway Commission. *Enterprise Risk Management Framework.* 1994. Reprinted with permission of AICPA.
2. MacKenzie, Kenneth D. *Organizational Design: The Organizational Audit and Analysis Technology.* Norwood, NJ: Ablex Publishing Corp., 1986.

BIBLIOGRAPHY

ANSI/ISO/ASQ Q9000-2000. *American National Standard: Quality Management Systems.* Milwaukee: American Society for Quality, 2000.

Aristotle. *Metaphysics.* Book III. University of Chicago: Great Books, 1952.

Britannica World Language Dictionary, Chicago: Encyclopaedia Britannica, Inc. 1959.

Enterprise Risk Management Framework. Committee of Sponsoring Organizations of the Treadway Commission, 2004. *www.coso.org.*

Faulkner, Harold. *American Political and Social History.* New York: Appleton, 1952.

Goldscheider, Ludwig. *Michelangelo: Paintings; Sculpture; Architecture.* London: Phaidon Publishers. Monochrome plates, including the *Madonna of Bruges,* copyright of Clarke and Sherwell, Ltd. 1953.

Halliday, D. and R. Resnick. *Physics for Students of Science and Engineering.* New York: John Wiley, 1964.

ISO 9000: Quality Management Standard. International Organization for Standardization, 2004. Milwaukee: American Society for Quality.

IT Control Objectives for Sarbanes-Oxley. IT Governance Institute and the Information Systems Audit and Control Association, 2004. *www.isaca.org.*

Lochner, Robert, and Joseph Matar. *Designing for Quality.* Milwaukee: ASQ Quality Press, 1990.

OCEG Framework. Open Compliance and Ethics Group, 2004. *www.oceg.org.*

Plato. *The Republic.* Book X. University of Chicago: Great Books, 1952.

Policy Governance Model. International Policy Governance Association, 2004. *www.ipga.org.*

Principles of Corporate Governance. Organization for Economic Cooperation and Development, 2004. *www.oecd.org.*

Public Company Accounting Reform and Investor Protection Act of 2002. HR 3763, 107th Congress of the United States of America, 2002. Short title: Sarbanes-Oxley Act of 2002.

INDEX

A
American National Standards Institute (ANSI) 41
American Society for Quality (ASQ) 35, 41
ANAB *see* ANSI-ASQ National Accreditation Board
Andersen, Arthur 49, 50, 52, 53
ANSI *see* American National Standards Institute
ANSI-ASQ National Accreditation Board (ANAB) 41, 42, 88, 89, 90, 92, 93, 94, 95, 98
ASQ *see* American Society for Quality
audit, external 91, 95; independent 91; internal 91, 95, 106; third-party 90, 91, 94, 95
auditor independence 51, 52–56, 57, 88, 90, 91–95, 97

B
benchmark processes 29
benchmarking 37, 42
best practices 36, 107, 110–111
Black Belt 34, 35, 47
Bridgestone/Firestone 6, 13

C
California Public Employees Retirement System (CalPERS) 53

CalPERS *see* California Public Employees Retirement System
certified public accountant (CPA) 54, 55
cheating 6, 12
CobIT *see* Control Objectives for Information Technology
Committee of Sponsoring Organizations of the Treadway Commission (COSO) xiii, xiv, 24, 62, 63, 64, 65, 66, 68, 69, 72, 74, 75, 110; sponsors of xiii
Comptroller General 57, 94, 98
consulting 47, 52, 92, 93
contracting 20; process of 20, 21–22
contract xii, 14, 17–25, 46, 90, 106
control, of quality xii, 28, 30, 31, 42, 91, 105; standard of 36–37
Control Objectives for Information Technology (CobIT) 66–67, 110
COQ *see* cost of quality
COSO *see* Committee of Sponsoring Organizations of the Treadway Commission
cost of quality (COQ) xii, xiv, 80, 81–83, 84–86
CPA *see* certified public accountant
Crosby, Philip 33

D

Deming, W. Edwards 7, 8, 10, 13, 14, 33, 58; 14 points of 7, 58
design of experiments (DOE) 31, 32
DOE *see* design of experiments
Drucker, Peter 8

E

ethics xii, 1–3, 5–14, 23, 25, 51, 52, 56, 57, 61, 63, 71, 88, 90, 92, 93, 97, 101, 113
Enron 49, 52, 53, 57, 94, 99
European Economic Community 41

European Union 41
external audit 91, 95

F

fear 7, 8, 10, 13, 58, 99, 100
Feigenbaum, Armand 14
Ford Motor Co. 6, 13, 75
form xii, 29–30, 47, 48
fraud 12, 49, 51, 58, 59, 89, 96, 98–100, 101

G

GAO *see* General Accounting Office
GATT *see* General Agreement on Tariffs and Trade
GDP *see* gross domestic product
GE Fanuc xiii, 46–47
General Accounting Office (GAO) 53, 54
General Agreement on Tariffs and Trade (GATT) 41
General Motors 54
goodwill 1–3, 12, 67
Green Belt 34
gross domestic product (GDP) 31

I

independent audit 91
Information Systems Audit and Control Association (ISACA) 66
information technology (IT) 20, 23, 24, 66–67, 96, 104, 106, 107, 110, 111, 112
integration, of systems 72–75
internal audit 91, 95, 106
Internal Revenue Service 49
International Organization for Standardization (ISO) 41
inventory 2, 67, 83–84, 85
ISACA *see* Information Systems Audit and Control Association

ISO *see* International Organization for Standardization
IT *see* information technology
IT Governance Institute (ITGI) 24, 66
ITGI *see* IT Governance Institute

J
just-in-time 84

K
kaizen 31

L
lean 6, 7, 31, 35–36, 66

M
Malcolm Baldrige National Quality Award (MBNQA) 32, 33, 35, 66
Malcolm Baldrige program 31
management, resource 3, 111; risk 62, 67, 68, 84; total quality (TQM) 31, 32–33
Master Black Belt 34, 47
materiality 59, 85
MBNQA *see* Malcolm Baldrige National Quality Award

N
National Commission on Fraudulent Financial Reporting xiii

O
Occupational Safety and Health Administration (OSHA) 76
OECD *see* Organization for Economic Cooperation and Development
operational framework 72
Organization for Economic Cooperation and Development (OECD) 24, 28

OSHA *see* Occupational Safety and Health Administration
Oxley, Michael 50

P
paper trail 45, 46
PCAOB *see* Public Company Accounting Oversight Board
performance standard xiii, 18, 23, 24, 28, 36
performer xii, 8, 11, 12, 17–25, 33, 85, 96, 104, 105
President's Corporate Fraud Task Force 99
preventive action 83
prison xii, xiv, 2, 10, 46, 85, 88, 105
Process Owner 34, 91, 93, 107, 108, 109, 110, 111
Public Company Accounting Oversight Board (PCAOB) 51–52, 54, 88, 90, 96
Public Company Accounting Reform and Investor Protection Act of 2002 5, 50, 103

Q
QA *see* quality assurance
QMS *see* quality management system
quality, control of xii, 28, 30, 31, 42, 91, 105; cost of (COQ) xii, xiv, 80, 81–83, 84–86; standard of 32, 39–40, 41; system of 28–29, 30, 33, 41, 43, 68, 69, 76, 85, 96, 97, 100, 101, 104–105, 106; toolbox of 30–31, 32, 105
quality assurance (QA) 41
Quality Leader 34, 36, 37
quality management, standard of 19, 28–30; total (TQM) 31, 32–33
quality management system (QMS) xii, xiii, xiv, 27–37, 41, 42, 43, 44, 73, 75, 76, 88, 90, 95, 96

R

RAB *see* Registrar Accreditation Board
Registrar Accreditation Board (RAB) 92
regulatory requirement 22, 72, 73, 76
requirement, regulatory 22, 72, 73, 76; statutory 73, 76
resource management 3, 111
risk management 62, 67, 68, 84

S

Sarbanes, Paul 50
SEC *see* Securities and Exchange Commission
Securities and Exchange Act of 1934 58, 100
Securities and Exchange Commission (SEC) xiii, 28, 49, 50, 51, 54, 57, 62, 90, 96, 98
self-assessment 37, 42
Shewhart, Walter 40
Shewhart control chart 28, 68
Six Sigma xiii, 5, 6, 7, 31, 33–36, 47, 66; DMAIC process of 75; hierarchical structure of 34
SOX titles xii, xiii, xiv, 50–59, 88–101
specification xii, 17–25, 45
SQC *see* statistical quality control
standard 17–25; of control 36–37; of performance xiii, 18, 23, 24, 28, 36; of quality 32, 39–40, 41; of quality management 19, 28–30
statistical quality control 28, 31, 32
statutory requirement 73, 76
substance 29–30, 48
system, of quality 28–29, 30, 33, 41, 43, 68, 69, 76, 85, 96, 97, 100, 101, 104–105, 106; of quality management (QMS) xii, xiii, xiv, 27–37, 41, 42, 43, 44, 73, 75, 76, 88, 90, 95, 96
systems integration 72–75

T

Taguchi, Genichi 3
Taguchi methods 31
Taylor, Frederick W. 9
third-party audit 90, 91, 94, 95
titles, of SOX xii, xiii, xiv, 50–59, 88–101
toolbox, of quality 30–31, 32, 105
total quality management (TQM) 31, 32–33
Toyota Production System 31, 35
TQM *see* total quality management

U

U.S. Navy 13, 19, 22, 24, 40

V

value-adding 6, 12, 36, 80

W

Watson, Tom 8, 13
whistle-blowing 12, 13, 58, 59
World War II 40, 41

Z

zero defects 33